YOUR GOLDEN JOURNEY

....

A 45-DAY PILGRIMAGE TO PERSONAL TRANSFORMATION

DIANA CHRISTINSON

PEN & PUBLISH
SAINT LOUIS, MISSOURI

Copyright ©2021 Diana Christinson

All rights reserved. No part of this book may be reproduced or transmitted in any form or by any means, electronic or mechanical, including photocopying, recording, or by any information storage and retrieval system, without permission in writing from the publisher.

Published by Pen & Publish, LLC, USA

www.PenandPublish.com
info@PenandPublish.com

Saint Louis, Missouri
(314) 827-6567

EXCEPTION: "Signs and Symptoms of Inner Peace™"
excerpted from "Symptoms of Inner Peace™"
By Saskia Davis © 1984
For reprint permission contact: symptomsofinnerpeace@gmail.com
http://www.symptomsofinnerpeace.net/Home.html

Book and journal design by Lorna Moy-Masaki.

Mountain path art by Torky at www.Dreamstime.com.

Back cover photo by Stephen Orlick.

Paperback ISBN: 978-0-9844600-6-9

e-book ISBN: 978-1-956897-00-5

Library of Congress Control Number: 2021920391

Publisher's Cataloging-in-Publication data

Christinson, Diana

    Your Golden Journey : a 45-day pilgrimage to personal transformation / Diana Christinson
    p. cm.
    Includes references.
    ISBN 978-0-9844600-6-9

LC Subjects 1. Self-actualization 2. Conduct of Life 3. Self-Realization

Other Subjects (BISAC) 1. SELF-HELP / Motivational & Inspirational 2. SELF-HELP / Personal Growth / Happiness 3. SELF-HELP / Personal Growth / Success

BJ1589 .M259 2021

LC record available at https://lccn.loc.gov/2021920391

DDC 158.1 2021920391

1st edition, November 2021

Printed on acid-free paper.

DEDICATION

During creation there was placed within your soul a vision. It is your only mission in this lifetime to go within and retrieve it. You are on a glorious quest to realms where imagination shall reign supreme, but it is through your heart that you will be shown the way.

—DORIEN ISRAEL

Dedicated to my father,

HOWARD PAUL BURNS,
a true visionary.

Your visions extended beyond what was in front of you.
You saw possibility.
And with unwavering courage, you lived that possibility,
you lived your dreams.

May I follow in your footsteps.
Blessed am I to love you forever.

The Hero

My father, whom I lovingly call Papa, was my hero and still is to this day. He had a troubled childhood; his sister died of pneumonia when he was three. His parents divorced soon after; the placement of blame for his sister's death had become an issue. He grew up fending for himself and was often in trouble, and by age ten, young Howard was sent to a home for "delinquent youth." He was there from ten till fourteen. He did not graduate high school but instead enrolled in the Air Force at fifteen (his date of birth forged by his mother on the required paperwork). His early years were only the beginning of a story of a man who overcame his challenges.

I was thirteen when the original Rocky movie was released. Our family, with dogs in tow, went to see the movie at the drive-in theater in our VW van. I can still hear Rocky's theme song playing through the sound box in the van window. My father was Rocky; he was the underdog, the person no one expected to succeed. They were wrong.

He worked hard, followed his dreams, and was a risk-taker unafraid of failure. A loving husband and father, he was also an entrepreneur with a vision. He opened our family restaurant, where we worked together as a family, and these were happy years.

Later in life, we learned my father had Huntington's disease. In his seventies, he could no longer drive; soon after, he could no longer ride a bike or swim, and eventually, he could not walk or get out of bed on his own. Through it all, his positive attitude never wavered. As his body changed, his attitude did not. Always, always, he was optimistic, making the most of each day. His favorite saying: "I'm a lucky man." I grew up hearing this mantra and was blessed to hold his hand during his passing and hear him whisper, "I am a lucky man."

Over the years, I observed the way my father turned a vision into a reality. By his example and with his unwavering encouragement, he instilled in me a passion for life. He inspired me to see life as an adventure, to take risks, and to not be afraid of failure. Through osmosis, I took on his strong character, his lens of optimism, and his passion for life.

I believe we are all faced with challenges at times and are called to overcome them. I chose to study psychology because I wanted to share my belief that we can create the life we choose.

Today, I share my father's message with you:

- We are the heroes and heroines of our stories.
- Life can be a great adventure.
- Challenges can encourage us to grow, to change, to find the opportunities. To feel blessed and lucky.
- You make your path.

May this Golden Journey awaken your sense of adventure and remind you that YOU are the hero or heroine of your story. Lucky you.

The Angel

My mother was raised in a Catholic home, attended parochial school, entered the convent at seventeen, and left three years later. She later married my dad and brought my brother and me into this wonderful, marvelous world.

In my youth, I loved my horse, my motorcycle, hiking, track—your typical teen. I also had a special influencer, my mother. When I was young, she molded and taught me the importance of inner beauty, to know myself and live every part of me from the inside out.

Lessons learned from my mother:

- Start and end the day with prayer or reflection (with or without spoken words).
- Be kind.
- Be grateful as much and often as possible.
- Be still and find silence to hear the voice within.

- Find ways and reasons to celebrate.
- Feel/seek awe and wonder.
- Laugh. Laugh so hard your sides hurt and you get the laughing farts or even pee your pants!
- Believe in miracles, and expect miracles.
- Believe in magic.
- Keep it simple.
- Appreciate the beauty of this world—the butterflies, the sun, moon, and stars.
- Love is the greatest gift.

A daily morning sacred time is my inheritance. As early as I can remember, my mom began every day with devotion (and still does today). I took on this practice as a young woman and, like my mom, continue to this day. It is my place to quiet my busy mind, to stand still long enough to hear my heart. It has been my strength through life's inevitable challenges, the practice allows me to live my beauty from the inside.

At eighty, my mom continues her daily sacred morning and evening devotions. She meditates, reads spiritual books, and prays for friends, both hers and mine. She continues to believe in magic, feel awe, and celebrate the miracles of nature and of love. I not only continue my morning devotion but have passed this on to my students. In this forty-five-day journey, you will create your own sacred morning devotion, cultivating your inner beauty and strength. Some friends refer to my mom as an angel, and there may well be earth angels. I think perhaps an angel has invited you to begin your forty-five-day golden journey, a time for growth and transformation.

The Muse

I met Anna May while working at the Laura's House domestic violence shelter. It was a typical nonprofit and my first job out of graduate school: I had three titles and five jobs. Anna May and I created programs, and together, we led unique learning opportunities for the women at the shelter. She was feisty, spoke her mind, and had her advanced degrees from the University of Life. We hit it off immediately, continued as colleagues, and became friends, and eventually, I began my personal work with her as my life coach. She led me, inspired me, and kicked my butt when it came to pursuing my dreams and navigating my relationships, my career, and my business. She set the bar high, confronting my fears and questioning my decisions, and she believed in me in a way that allowed me to fail and get back up until my dreams were my reality.

Teaching was and is my great love. Anna May knew that I would eventually gather my teachings, sift through them, put pen to paper, and write a book. One day during a session, she announced, "I have the title for your first book; it's one word. Are you curious?" She had my attention.

The title: DO

The tagline: **Transforming Your Life through Practice**

She nailed it. Anna May knew and inspired my strong belief in doing.

Thank you, Anna May.

In loving memory of my coach, friend, and muse.

TABLE OF CONTENTS

YOUR FORTY-FIVE-DAY PILGRIMAGE TO PERSONAL TRANSFORMATION

The Story of Our Seal
Our Seal
Your Guide
An Invitation
Your Golden Journey
The Meaning behind Your Golden Journey
Your Golden Practice

Day 1: Locate Yourself
Day 2: Follow Your Passions
Day 3: Mastering Gratitude
Day 4: Breathe with Your Nose, Eat with Your Mouth
Day 5: Unplug and Reset
Day 6: Space Training
Day 7: Catch a Thought and Flip It
Day 8: Imaginal Cells
Day 9: Travel Light
Day 10: I Make My Path

Day 11: Move the Furniture
Day 12: Peace Out
Day 13: Artist in You
Day 14: I Am the Master
Day 15: Choose Happiness
Day 16: Energy Banking
Day 17: Get Up and Move
Day 18: Give a Smile
Day 19: Nature's Medicine
Day 20: Forest Bathing

Day 21: Barn's Burnt Down
Day 22: Lucky Me!
Day 23: Wild Life
Day 24: Giving Bread
Day 25: A Healthy Mental Diet
Day 26: A Garland of Gratitude
Day 27: Bring the Outdoors In
Day 28: Dancing in the Rain
Day 29: The Invitation
Day 30: Reach for the Sun

Day 31: Wabi-Sabi
Day 32: Kintsugi
Day 33: Plant a Garden
Day 34: If Not Now, When?
Day 35: Lose Your Shoes
Day 36: The Invisible Gift
Day 37: How We Spend Today
Day 38: What If?
Day 39: Awaken from Your Sensory Slumber
Day 40: The We of Me

Day 41: A Message from a Wasp
Day 42: Influencers
Day 43: Happiness Is an Inside Job
Day 44: Love and Happiness
Day 45: You Are the Hero

The Gift
Day 46: The Journey Continues

One Thousand Gratitudes
References

The Story of Our Seal

The seal script is the ancestor of modern standard characters. Ancient characters have even and thin lines that don't look like brush strokes because they were created during the time when "writing" was carving on bones, metal, or other hard materials, before paper and brushes were invented. So using seal script is actually more reflective of history. The seal character stamps are traditionally deemed the official form and perceived as authoritative and artistic. —ANDY CHUANG

While living in Kyoto, Japan, I used the red traditional seal as a way to sign my name. In Japan, your name or the name of your business is part of your story, your ancestry and history. I love the image of a word and found that translating English into Japanese brought more meaning and essence to each name. I became fascinated with translations and how they deepen my understanding.

Your Golden Journey is more than a book. It is a process of introspection and simple practices that leads to personal growth and transformation. I had the title translated into Japanese to express the essence, the true nature, of the meaning.

Andy Chuang translated:

Journey—also used as road/path to represent our life history and future

Golden—representing the quality of the journey that would lead to transformation

Heart (your/personal)—was translated to *heart* to signify the inward and personal aspect of the journey

Andy created a new character, *The Gold Heart*, which translates to:

This Journey Will Reach Personal Transformation.

YOUR GOLDEN JOURNEY TO TRANSFORMATION

We all have our internal/inner/heart journeys
(character: heart)

Then we come to your Golden Journey
(character: gold) 金 **(gold/golden)**

And through this journey we'll reach personal transformation
(gold+heart: a new character)

金　(gold/golden)
路　(road/path)
歷程　(journey/process)
金路歷程　(golden journey; journey of gold)

Your Guide

The longest, most exciting journey is the journey inward. — KONSTANTIN STANISLAVSKI

If you asked me today, "Who are you?" I would respond with a grin on my face: "I am a lover of life and people." I see life as an adventure, and I believe that the hardships are as much a part of our journey as the joys. I have experienced and witnessed the power of inspiration on people's ability to grow and transform, and my years of living and teaching health practices have reaffirmed my belief that we can change, heal, and grow from the inside out.

My life passions and travels have taken me to far-off places and opened many doors along the way. My journey includes lessons from ancient philosophy, world religions, human psychology and physiology, and universal truths. My path also includes friendly monks, wise gurus, mentors and muses, and love and devotion to nature's miracles. One of my favorite heroines, Isak Dinesen, wrote of her years living on her coffee plantation at the Ngong Hills outside of Nairobi in her memoir *Out of Africa*. She was a strong, brave woman and thirsty for exploration. She adapted to life in a foreign land by learning from her experiences, friends, and mistakes. Dinesen inspired me not only to travel but to work and live in Asia.

After graduating from college, while my friends found jobs and began their careers, I set off to experience, explore, and teach in Japan. I embarked on my journey alone, leaving behind my safe and familiar life. With a suitcase, a plane ticket, and a sense of adventure, I left for Kyoto. Living in Japan was a dream, and I loved the temples, gardens, culture, and people. I immersed myself in my studies of Zen meditation and read Japanese philosophy and poetry. My hope was to weave together my passions for psychology and Eastern philosophy with holistic health modalities.

After a year, I had an opportunity to continue my Asian travels in Thailand. Again, I traveled alone. Everything I needed for this part of my journey fit into the purple backpack my Japanese friends had given me. I had a one-way ticket to Bangkok and a job interview with a relief and development organization, Food for the Hungry. My plan was to stay for a year, immerse myself in the culture, and study Thai Buddhism. I was offered the job and spent a year in a small village on the border with Cambodia, with Khmer Rouge soldiers still near and land mines around the rice fields. While I needed to be careful when leaving the compound, my room on stilts over water, topped with a thatch roof, became my very own Walden Pond. I felt connected to nature and to the people, and I learned to live simply and be of service to those in need. Every gesture of giving repaid me tenfold and filled me with abundant joy.

During my years in Thailand and Japan, I met many characters and made new and unexpected friends. My time abroad had changed me. I had traveled to experience the culture and values of the Japanese and Thai people, but I had also acquired new skills, utilized my strengths, collected life lessons, and learned about myself. These two years taught me more than any formal education or books, and this powerful time of my life was transformative, leaving a lasting imprint on the woman I have become.

Following my years in Asia, I pursued my passion to serve and support the community back home. I utilized my degree in psychology to direct and plan programs at youth shelters and inner city after-school programs. After working with individuals and community programs for people with mental illnesses and developmental disabilities, I decided to further my education and earned an MA in psychology. My dream was to integrate my love for Eastern culture and philosophy with the new, developing field of positive psychology and neuroscience.

I was ready for another adventure. My interest in health sciences and Asian philosophy called me to India, where I stayed for one to three months at a time. It was my personal pilgrimage to study with master yoga teachers. India became my special yearly retreat, and I traveled to South India annually for ten years. I continued my education in yoga, yoga philosophy, breath practices, and Ayurvedic medicine.

In 2004, I opened a yoga school named Pacific Ashtanga Yoga Shala. In Sanskrit, one of the oldest languages in the world, *shala* means school. My vision was to bring my students holistic health through yoga, philosophy, meditation, and breath work. Through classes, teachings, and workshops, I integrate practices for the three bodies: physical, energetic, and spiritual. I still enjoy developing and teaching our semester studies, which include weekly conferences on traditional yoga teachings combined with Eastern and Western philosophies and psychology.

This book is a collection of knowledge gained over years of teaching, coaching, and living. I have shared these teachings as a guest lecturer for local university students, in seminars I've led, and when working with individuals as a life coach, supporting and guiding people seeking growth and change.

Your Golden Journey is an opportunity to study these powerful teachings and to remind you that you are the star, writer, and hero or heroine of your life. While I love traveling, I have learned that you don't have to go to foreign countries to have a transformative adventure; the true journey is within. Today, dear friends, both literature and life experience continue to inspire me to live life as an adventure. All the places, people, and experiences along your daily path are opportunities to awaken your inner golden self.

As your guide and teacher on this journey, I want you to know: If you are holding this book, I believe our life paths were meant to cross. I believe if you are thirsty for inspiration, you will find it. If you are willing and open to growth and change, this journey will transform you. I believe that life is a gift and an extraordinary adventure.

Blessings to you on your Golden Journey to transformation.

Your guide & teacher,
Diana

An Invitation

The journey of a thousand miles begins with one step. —LAO TZU

I invite you to take your first step on an inward journey of self-discovery and awakening. *Your Golden Journey* is a six-week self-study experience filled with meditation, inspiration, and self-reflection. Through daily teachings weaving Eastern philosophy and culture with Western psychology, you will be guided to cultivate more peace, joy, and mindful presence in the moments of your life.

Fill your cup with dedicated sacred time for you. Fifteen minutes of quiet allows you to turn inward and connect with yourself. Read and reflect on practices that will influence how you show up for the precious moments of your day.

> *Self-care is never a selfish act—it is only good stewardship of the only gift I have, the gift I was put on earth to offer others.*
> —Parker J. Palmer

Join me on this personal heart journey. Mark your calendar *DAY ONE* and highlight each day through day forty-five. You will be encouraged to get outside, retrain your breath, Flip a Thought, and create more space in between life happening and you responding. By utilizing practices for vibrant, healthy living for your body, energy, and emotional health, this forty-five-day pilgrimage will transform your way of living.

Your daily Golden Practice is a gift you offer yourself that provides nourishment through quiet stillness and inspiration through reading and reflective journaling. You will set intentions, create new habits, become a skilled observer, and begin to shift your habitual thought patterns.

> *The Chinese have a simple saying,* yi ke qian jin, *which means: time is gold; every moment counts.*

Nourish your spirit, fill your cup, grow, and acquire new skills that will assist you in how you show up for the great adventure—and the precious moments—of your life.

The Meaning behind Your Golden Journey

As you move toward a dream, the dream moves toward you... —JULIA CAMERON

Our entire life journey is a culmination of many smaller ones. Think of times you have set an intention to improve your health, inspire creativity, or change an old pattern. We sign up for a membership at a gym, hire a personal trainer, or start a new diet. We read an inspirational book or work with a life coach to guide us in the changes we hope to make. Often it is a birthday, anniversary, or new year when we choose to set an intention to change. Other times, it may be a trauma or setback that is the catalyst to devote time to ourselves. This six-week pilgrimage is an opportunity to make a commitment to yourself, to devote time and energy to set goals and achieve more vibrant health.

Journey

A journey is defined as an act of traveling or a passage. It is not only the places but also the life experience. The journey of our life may include the places we lived or visited, but a journey is also the path of life as expressed in experiences. Our history is mapped out with many small journeys. Our life is our great journey.

When we step back to view life as a great journey, we can identify the many paths, stories, and life situations that brought us to the present day. I like to think of our life path as the hero's journey, as described by Joseph Campbell, and to view our personal stories in the bigger universal picture of life's adventures and opportunities for exploration.

Gold

The golden sun rises each morning, and the world lights up one corner at a time. We begin a new day filled with possibility. *Golden* represents the possibilities that each morning, each day, holds for us. In every culture, gold is valued as the highest commodity. *A golden opportunity* is a rewarding one, a potential springboard to greatness. We adorn winners with gold medals to identify the very best. Spiritual practices, sages, and philosophers refer to our inner self as being golden or refer to the gold within us. Alchemy transforms base metals into gold. To journey inward is to discover and embrace our true value and potential, our internal Golden Self.

This journey of gold is an inward exploration to awaken and tap into your inner reservoir, to call on your highest qualities, and to honor and respect yourself. By devoting time to finding the golden qualities already within you, you will embark on a personal excavation to discover your golden potential to live your life with more peace, joy, happiness, and love.

Transformation

For thousands of years, people have been going on pilgrimages for personal growth and transformation. These pilgrims leave the comfort of home, family, and work to travel, but not to vacation, sightsee, rest, or retreat. The goal of traveling is to change and improve. The journey we will take together, which has no religious affiliations, has the potential to be a light on your path of personal spirituality.

Transformation is shifting to a simple way of being. We find more balance with work and play; we increase our happiness and decrease our anxiety and worry. We release control and experience less irritation and more joy. We seek transformation to change how we show up for the moments of our life.

We do one thing or another; we stay the same, or we change.
Congratulations, if you have changed.
—Mary Oliver

Your *Golden* Journey is an inspiration and reminder to live your potential, your joy, your adventure today.

Your Golden Practice

The key is in not spending time, but in investing it.

—STEPHEN R. COVEY

In today's fast-paced world, it's easy to find yourself repeating the mantra *I don't have enough time. I am too busy.* Our day gives us twenty-four hours; sixteen to seventeen of those are spent awake. How many of those hours are spent working, busy, running? How much time is devoted to self-care? I invite you to join me for a fifteen-minute practice that will give the other twenty-three and three-quarters hours of your day more energy, perspective, and peace.

Your First Mental Meal of the Day:

Do you remember hearing that your first meal of the day is the most important and being encouraged to eat fresh fruit and oat bran? How we fuel our body with food is how we fill our tank for the day. Mental "food" is equally, if not more, important. Beginning our day with positive, hopeful, happy thoughts fills our minds with healthy fuel for the day.

Fifteen minutes of sacred silence, inspiration, and reflection is *your first meal of the day* before consuming news, emails, texts, or social media. You may choose to reflect silently, journal your thoughts, or both. Besides a journal and pen, consider adding special colored pens, crayons, or paint to your space. This is your time to welcome creativity! Bring and enjoy a cup of coffee or tea, and invite your dogs or cat to snuggle next to you. Surround yourself with what makes this time sacred and your own. *First*, fill your cup with energy and inspiration, *then* go out into your day.

The time is ideally in the morning before you start your daily routine of doing, before you check your phone for work or news. Practicing at the same time each day will provide consistency and add to the feeling of respecting yourself by gifting yourself time. Whatever time works best for you is perfect—morning, midday, or evening. The time you choose is less important than you making daily time for yourself.

The place can be any room in your home or office. You can sit in a chair or on a meditation cushion. Use a shelf, table, or counter to create a sacred space where you can light a candle, ring a bell or chime, light incense, or use essential oils. Add a plant, a picture, or a vase with fresh flowers to your space. You might include a compass to remind you of this journey along your life path. Use simple items that are meaningful to you, and create a sacred place that is uniquely yours.

This is a special time for an inward journey of self-expansion, growth, and transformation. A helpful tip for this journey is to ask your family to honor this time. You can also share your time with your partner and family if that works best for you. Growing up and seeing my mom during her morning devotion, I recognized at a young age that we honored her special time. Observing her practice became an unspoken gift that I have incorporated into my life as my own daily morning devotion.

Your Daily Golden Practice

Your daily Golden Practice is your time for practicing presence, connecting with yourself, listening to your heart, and nurturing your spirit. This is your opportunity to create and experience sacred time each day.

The Sacred

Your sacred space is where you can find yourself again and again.
—Joseph Campbell

When something is deserving of reverence and respect, it is considered sacred. How would you define *sacred*? What is sacred to you? Many things can be sacred: a promise, a place, an experience, or a ritual that brings us a feeling of internal reverence. I believe we are designed to experience and feel sacred moments as a way to cultivate deeper meaning and value in our lives. You may have felt the depth of reverence when you entered a cathedral or a temple or witnessed a brilliant sunrise. We create the same feeling with ritual. Candles, the sound of a bell, and the smell of incense awaken the sacred within us.

Self-Study

Svadhyaya is a Sanskrit term that translates as *sva*, meaning "self," and *adhyaya,* meaning "getting close to something." It is the act of getting close to yourself.

The journey inward is an opportunity to spend time listening to your innermost self and voice that is often drowned out with the noise of our busy lives. Self-study is an important practice often neglected. Your Golden Journey is a daily opportunity to create time for yourself and serves as a guide to discovering new ways to observe, listen, and live. The path you walk will be your time of silence, daily reading, and reflection.

Intention

Sankalpa is a Sanskrit term which translates as "to resolve or do," "to achieve an objective," or "a vow or solemn promise to oneself."

Begin this time of self-study with intention. My intention for you is that you will create a practice that belongs to you—a sacred time to fill your cup, give you energy, and inspire how you live the precious moments of your life. Set your intention as self-care, or add something personal to this time on your journey. You may want to gain personal insight, increase happiness and decrease stress, ignite your creativity, or rekindle passion in a relationship. Set some time to listen, and set your intention to make a commitment and a vow to yourself. Any time you improve yourself, you improve your life.

Touchstone

Using a physical symbol as a reminder on your forty-five-day journey can deepen your experience on the journey. Many traditions use a simple cotton thread around the wrist as a reminder of a special intention or commitment. Over the years, I have taken rituals from different cultures and practices to create meaningful reminders of ways to encourage change. For years, I brought back with me thread blessed in a temple in India to share with my students on their anniversaries, birthdays, and holidays to deepen the intention. When my dear friend Chusang Rinpoche visits from Nepal, I ask him to bring blessed prayer thread for my students. On one of his visits, he called to tell me he had found the best prayer threads at a place in New York called Michaels. I laughed, but it was beautiful to realize that all of our precious threads had come from a craft store. It is the intention we place in the cotton thread on our wrist that makes it meaningful to us. A wedding band is a piece of metal, but it is the vow and promise of love that give the wedding band its meaning.

As an added reminder of your journey, you may choose to find a thread and make or buy a cotton bracelet. You can wear a *mala* or a special, significant piece of jewelry. While not required, it is an additional ritual you may wish to add to your Golden Journey.

There is *no* wrong way to do your Golden Practice.

As mentioned before, the preferable time to practice is in the golden hours of the morning before you connect with the outside world. If you miss the morning, practice at lunch or in the evening. If some days you only have five minutes to unplug and breathe and go within, it will still offer you a moment of peaceful self-connection. Complete your reading, reflection, and practice with grace rather than self-judgment. Make this experience work for you, and celebrate the big and little shifts you begin to notice along the way. The most important thing is to gift yourself a daily loving, inspiring practice.

Enjoy the journey.

YOUR GOLDEN PRACTICE

Sit down in a comfortable seated position—
this could be in a chair or on the floor.

RELAX

With a long spine, relax your shoulders—
soft and down, away from your ears.

CENTERED, AT EASE

Breathe gently through your nose several times.

IN AND OUT
IN AND OUT
IN AND OUT
RELAX

Close your eyes or gaze at a candle.
Slow down your breath.
Let everything go.
Let go of all tension in your body.
And let go of all your thoughts and inner dialogues.
Just sit. Just breathe. Just be.

There is nothing to figure out, no one to impress, nothing to prove.
Experience the joy and peace of meditation.

Enjoy a sacred silence for three to five minutes (or longer—your choice).

Read the Daily Inspiration.
Reflect and Journal.
Incorporate practices into your day.

BONUS:
Visit www.DianaChristinson.com to enjoy a sound-bath
meditation and incorporate it into your Golden Practice.

DAY 1
Locate Yourself

Man cannot discover new oceans unless he has the courage to lose sight of the shore.
— ANDRÉ GIDE

Deep in the forest, the trees grow thick and the trail thin. I can no longer see the ridge of the mountain. I am lost. Realizing I am off the trail, I reach in my pocket for my compass. I stop; hold the compass in my palm, parallel with my chest; watch the pin; and still my hand. I need to locate myself. I am reading the magnet for north to find my way back to the trail and navigate my way through the forest.

How many times have I lost my way? The forest of life has many unexpected turns. Off my life course, I stop walking, doing. I stand still to find my true north, to locate myself. Once I know where I am—once I have stilled my own jumping, jittering heart pin—I connect to my internal navigation and my heart's true north. My internal compass leads me back to my path.

As a young woman fresh out of college, my first trip abroad was not a vacation but a job teaching English in Kyoto, Japan. The first month of my new adventure did not go as planned. My apartment was not ready. I was living with a kind family who served fish and seaweed soup for breakfast (I do not like fish or seaweed). With lots of house noise, city noise, and zero privacy, I was missing donuts and silence and questioning my decision. One night, I went up to the apartment rooftop by myself, above the loud, busy city noise below, and found my place of peace. I will always remember that night. I stood looking out over the city and located myself as I sat with my unhappiness and disappointment. In the silence, I found my true north, my inner strength, my will and ability to navigate through feeling lost in a foreign country. I found my way and am grateful I stayed, as Japan remains one of my great life adventures. My true north did not fail me.

My friend Jay is a geologist who has traveled all over the world with his compass as a guide on many adventures. The compass always points and shows us the north pole; on land or sea, it helps us find our way home. Inspired by the powerful metaphor of the compass and our ability to navigate through life knowing our true north, I asked Jay to tell me everything he knew and loved about the compass. I am not sure who was more excited, he to share or I to learn, about this powerful but simple device. I had my journal and pen, and as he spoke, I took notes.

> Notes from my afternoon with Jay, written with large letters and circled:
>
> LOCATE YOURSELF.
>
> STAND STILL. (You must stand still to locate yourself.)
>
> THE PIN SETTLES; THAT IS NORTH. (Your metaphorical internal pin settles; that is your true north.)
>
> WHEN YOU KNOW WHERE YOU ARE, YOU CAN SET A COURSE FOR WHERE YOU CHOOSE TO GO.

I was excited to create a teaching on the compass to share inspirations on how to navigate our way through life using this tool rich with history and deeper meaning. With no shortage of teachings and inspirations, I intertwined the concept of the compass with my teachings on Joseph Campbell's *The Hero's Journey* and the Camino pilgrimage, eventually developing an entire semester of teachings on the compass.

How many times have you been lost? How many more times will you feel you have lost your way on your path of life? Many? Many. It's okay—you have your internal compass. You know how to stand still, to quiet and settle your internal pin and find your true north. You can locate yourself and find your way back home or choose a new path, a new destination.

We all have stories of times when we felt lost. Our lives are daring, exciting, mysterious adventures. Take risks, lose sight of the shore, get lost. Know that you can always locate yourself. **Be still and wait—true north is within. It will not fail you.**

Reflection:

Do you remember a time when you stopped to locate yourself?

How did you choose to navigate from your true north?

Draw a red dot in your journal. Next to it, write I AM HERE. Map how you navigated through your forests and storms of life to be here today. Write out parts of your life story—your hero's journey—where you used your internal compass and true north to find your way.

Practice:

True North Meditation: Take five minutes or more to sit in silent meditation. Place your hands over your heart. Locate yourself and listen to your internal voice. (Also use this practice whenever feeling unsure about an important decision.)

Watch:

The Ancient Technique to Making Tough Decisions with Gregg Braden on www.DianaChristinson.com

YOUR GOLDEN JOURNEY
A 45-DAY PILGRIMAGE TO PERSONAL TRANSFORMATION

Follow Your Passions

Follow your bliss. If you do follow your bliss, you put yourself on the kind of track that has been there all the while waiting for you, and the life you are to be living is the one you are living. When you can see that, you begin to meet people who are in the field of your bliss, and they open the doors to you. I say, follow your lead and don't be afraid, and doors will open where you didn't know they were going to be. If you follow your bliss, doors will open for you that wouldn't have opened for anyone else.

— JOSEPH CAMPBELL

The stop sign on the road of life allows us to locate ourselves. We view the map of our life and see the big red dot, *I am here*. What led us here gives us a sense of our history, the path that brought us to today. The Greek philosopher Socrates expressed this in two words: *know thyself*. Our self-study *(svadhyaya)* sets the foundation from which we develop the dreams and intentions that get us off the couch of life where we are set in our familiar ways. Self-reflection awakens us to pursue our dreams and passions; it is a call to follow our bliss.

When I teach the Hero's Journey to a group or an individual, we begin with their stories. If I had a cup of coffee and a few hours with you, what would you tell me about your life story? How did you get here? What colors your story—heartbreak, adventure, discovery, your cast of characters? Who are the people, the sidekicks, the villains, who make up the pages of your life story? When setting a course, first ask: Where do you want to go? What are your dreams, passions, and loves? What do you get excited about? What stirs your soul?

As Joseph Campbell inspires us to follow our bliss, our destinations are often inspired by our passions and dreams. My love for Asia inspired a trip to Japan, my love for the ocean influenced me to make my home in Laguna, and my love for yoga brought me to studies in India.

My friend Alan left his life in Taiwan to live and study in the United States. While school wasn't his passion, cars were. Today, he's a successful artist and entrepreneur, designing unique car accessories.

My friend Merry loves nature and the environment. In her spare time, she volunteers as a docent at a local wildlife preserve, educating others on ways to appreciate and protect our environment.

My friend Maria is a real estate consultant by day, and by night she studies and enjoys salsa and flamenco dancing.

My UPS driver brings me fresh cucumbers from his plot at the local community garden, where he enjoys working the soil and watching things grow.

When we follow our passions and dreams as Joseph Campbell instructs us, doors will open to unexpected opportunities. An interest may lead to new places, new experiences and adventures. Your passions can influence how you map your course and how you unfold and enrich your future.

Reflection:

Reflect on the passions that brought you to where you are today.

Where do you want to go? What are your dreams, passions, and loves? What do you get excited about? What stirs your soul?

Make a list of two or three things that bring you joy, that ignite your passion.

Practice:

Pick one or two passions, and take steps to follow your bliss today. Here are some examples:

Interested in Asia? Start to learn a new language, read a book about Asian cultures, or visit a Japanese garden or tea house.

Foodie? Take a nightly cooking class. Invite friends over to try a new recipe. Meet your local farmers and learn about what it takes to grow your favorite produce.

Watch:

FINDING JOE: A story about Joseph Campbell and The Hero's Journey on www.DianaChristinson.com

DAY 3
Mastering Gratitude

Practice isn't the thing you do once you're good.
It's the thing you do that makes you good.
- MALCOLM GLADWELL

In his book *Outliers: The Story of Success*, Malcolm Gladwell shares his research and insight on the secrets to success. His work indicates that achievement can be attributed to the hours we put into practicing. How many hours? Gladwell writes, "Researchers have settled on what they believe is the magic number for true expertise: ten thousand hours." It makes sense; we get better at what we do and do repeatedly.

The compelling question is, *What is worth your ten thousand hours? What do you want to be good at?*

Pause to answer the question. Do you want to be successful in your work? Improve your golf or tennis game? Most of us would agree that we would like to be happy. In truth, what is more important than to cultivate happiness? Numerous research studies on happiness have shown that a simple, powerful way to create happiness is through gratitude.

> *"Gratitude is a powerful catalyst for happiness.*
> *It's the spark that lights a fire of joy in your soul."*
> *- Amy Collett*

Applying the 10,000 hour theory~

We become better at what we practice. How many hours would you put into learning to play a piece of music on the piano, learning three minutes of dance choreography, or learning a new language? By dedicating time each day to practicing being grateful and appreciative, we build pathways in our brains that train us to scan our world, as well as the moments of our lives, to see the blessings and feel the gratitude. The more we practice, the better we become.

> *"Neural pathways, comprised of neurons connected by dendrites, are created in the brain based on our habits and behaviors. The number of dendrites increases with the frequency a behavior is performed.*
> *- Julie Hani, "The Neuroscience of Behavior Change"*

We can change the way we think, feel, and live the moments of our days by training the mind. Wayne Dyer said, "If you change the way you look at things, the things you look at change." Practice scanning your days for people and experiences that bring you happiness, *then* add gratitude. On my drive to work, I might have missed the sun rising this morning, slowly casting light, waking the world from its darkness one tree at a time. I say, *I am grateful for the sun, the beauty of dawn, the trees*... When we PRACTICE gratitude daily, we begin to notice things we may have missed. I have dinner with a friend and observe myself smiling, laughing, feeling joy. Now I have raised my energy from happy to grateful to feeling blessed.

Practice:

Incorporate a Gratitude Meditation into your Golden Practice. Begin by holding your right hand over your heart. Touch each finger gently to your heart and name something you are grateful for—a person, thing, experience. Repeat as many times as you'd like to strengthen your ability to scan the world for blessings.

Your daily Gratitude Meditation will likely include many of the same people, experiences, or things each time (my family, my home, my health, my morning practice...). Continue refining your grateful lens by adding the *Pinky Practice*. For each hand of gratitude, the pinky is something new.

Reflection:

Create a gratitude journal and fill the pages with days, weeks, and years of practicing gratitude. Notice how this shifts your daily perspective. Observe how your energy and mental patterns change and happiness increases. After ten thousand hours of practicing Gratitude Meditation, your transformation will inspire you to continue this practice for the rest of your life.

Watch:

Join Diana for a led gratitude practice at www.DianaChristinson.com

DAY 4
Breathe with Your Nose, Eat with Your Mouth.

No matter what you eat, how much you exercise, how skinny or young or strong you are, none of it matters if you're not breathing properly.

- JAMES NESTOR

What's the best health advice I can give you after three decades of teaching yoga, meditation, breath training, and life coaching? *Breathe through your nose.*

My library is filled with yoga books on breath techniques that have kept people healthy for thousands of years. I have studied and trained using numerous breath techniques, but it doesn't take years of study to begin experiencing the proven health benefits from a simple breath practice. Breathing intentionally through the nose increases energy, sharpens brain function, increases physical performance, promotes relaxation, improves sleep, reduces anxiety, decreases stress, and reduces inflammation and pain. More recently, I've added to my library new books filled with research on breath as one of the top contributors to health or disease.

Science and medicine are now recognizing the value of not just *breathing* but *breathing correctly*. Breath is a major contributor to your overall health. Breathing is a part of the autonomic nervous system: we don't think about it, which means we are often unaware of *how* we are breathing and unaware that we're breathing incorrectly. Research shows that a possible eighty percent of the American population is breathing incorrectly, contributing to disease rather than health. Stop and think about this for a moment—that means that eight out of ten people are breathing incorrectly.

Not only do we need breath to survive, but the better we become at breathing efficiently, the healthier we will be. Consuming oxygen through the nose filters allergens and pollen and moisturizes and warms the air to body temperature, making it easier for your body to utilize oxygen. Nasal breathing also releases nitric oxide, which improves the circulation of oxygen in your body.

The *Optimal Breath* is a long, slow, smooth breath (without struggle) through the nose. The average person at rest breathes between eight and sixteen breaths per minute, while the ideal breath for health is to breathe less and longer, closer to eight breaths per minute. It turns out the *yoga breath* is the optimal way to breathe for overall health.

Breath expert Patrick McKeown has been studying, practicing, and teaching breath techniques for three decades. McKeown believes that breathing lightly and softly through the nose, using the diaphragm rather than the upper chest, calms the mind and improves the biochemistry of the body. In his book *The Oxygen Advantage*, he has taught functional breathing training intended to improve oxygen delivery and reduce breathlessness. These techniques alleviate asthma, anxiety, sleep apnea, nasal congestion, and more.

I teach methods of breathing as a form of medicine for people who suffer from both physical and emotional ailments. *Breathe through the nose, slow and long*. Taking just five long breaths immediately changes your body chemistry, which impacts your mood and physiology. Changing your health by breathing through your nose costs nothing and changes everything. Today, join me—breathe through your nose for optimal health.

Reflection:
Observe your own breath, as well as other people's breathing. Do you notice yourself and others breathing through the mouth?

Practice:
Incorporate breath training into your Golden Practice (preferably on an empty stomach).

Sit in a comfortable position or lie down.

Inhale through your nose, smoothly and softly, for the count of three (work up to five). Feel breath move up the spine to the top of your head, expanding the belly as air fills the bottom of the lungs.

Exhale through the nose, smoothly and softly, for the count of three (work up to five). Feel breath move down the spine, bringing the belly in as the lungs empty.

Take ten to fifteen full cycles of breath.

Get up carefully.

For Your Library:
Breath: The New Science of a Lost Art by James Nestor

The Oxygen Advantage by Patrick McKeown

Breathology: The Art Of Conscious Breathing by Stig Severinsen

Watch:
Let Diana lead you through a simple breath practice on www.DianaChristinson.com

Listen:
How The 'Lost Art' Of Breathing Can Impact Sleep And Resilience with Terry Gross and James Nestor on www.DianaChristinson.com

DAY 5
Unplug and Reset

Almost everything will work again if you unplug it for a few minutes, including you.
― ANNE LAMOTT

Have you ever had one of those days when the computer is down, the car battery died, the washer just flooded the back room, the maintenance person is out of town for two weeks, the deadline was yesterday, and you're on the phone for hours just trying to get the Wi-Fi to work? I was having one of those days: nothing was working. Then it came to me—advice from a friend: "Did you unplug it, turn it off for a few minutes, then turn it back on?" Something miraculous and magical happens when you do so: suddenly, and for no known reason, IT WORKS!

It turns out that what works for technology and electricity actually works for the body's wiring and circuitry too. When we unplug and reset, we feel refreshed. We can begin again with new perspective and vibrant, replenished energy.

Like our overheated computers and spotty Wi-Fi, our thinking selves, energetic selves, feeling selves become depleted, run down, stuck. We are physically and mentally fatigued from too much going and doing. If you've needed a sign, here it is:

STOP!

Actually *stop* what you are doing, take a few deep long breaths, take a break, move around the house or office.

Unplug—reset!

In 2016, a Nielsen audience report showed that adults in the United States spent about ten hours and thirty-nine minutes each day on digital devices (phones, tablets, computers, gaming devices, and TVs). That number has increased dramatically since then. According to Reid Health, studies have shown that adults who spend six or more hours per day watching screens have a higher risk for depression, and that "limiting social media use to 30 minutes per day leads to a 'significant improvement in well-being.'"

Part of unplugging is making the choice to turn off and *not back on*. Turn off and do something different. Go outside, listen to music, read a book. Decrease your time on devices and increase your energy and joy. I have been using this as a practice; certain times are now designated as *Off*. Walks in nature. *Off!* Having coffee with a friend. *Off!* Playtime with my dogs. *Off!*

Reflection:
Note how much time you spend on your devices.

How could you decrease your device time?

How could you increase your *Off* time?

Practice:
STOP - UNPLUG - RESET - OFF

Take small screen breaks throughout the day to breathe and reset.

Try leaving your phone out of reach to increase moments of mindful presence.

Watch:
Sleep is our most important daily reset! Watch Matt Walker's Ted Talk *Sleep is your Superpower* at www.DianaChristinson.com

DAY 6
Space Training

Between stimulus and response there is a space. In that space is our power to choose our response. in our response lies our growth and our freedom.

—VIKTOR FRANKL, MAN'S SEARCH FOR MEANING

I have memorized this Viktor Frankl quote; it is a personal mantra. These simple words inspire the way I show up for life. For me, *Space Training* is not about aerospace but rather training my own headspace. Frankl was a brilliant psychiatrist and used psychological language, such as stimulus and response. In simple terms, stimulus is life—not only what is actually happening but all the constant thoughts running through our heads. Response is how we react to whatever is happening, both in life and in our busy minds.

We do not have an off button; even when we sleep, our minds are producing thoughts. The truth is that most of the time we are on autopilot, completely unaware of our reactions to unconscious feelings and thoughts. It is that space between the two—*a pause*—in which we can create an opportunity to gain perspective and identify the stimulus. This gives us the opportunity to choose a response. It's like a magic doorway into your internal self that provides you with an opportunity to respond with thoughtful intention. You can choose to respond how you'd like—perhaps with more joy, compassion, and happiness. It is *in that choice of response* that we find true liberation and have the ability to grow and live the lives we want. Not just on the special days, but in those little moments that invite us to respond in ways that create more happiness and love in how we live the moments of our lives.

One day, a student, Troy, shared with me how Viktor Frankl's words and my teachings inspired by his book, *Man's Search for Meaning*, had recently changed his experience of surfing. He'd headed to the beach to go surfing, noticed the water was packed that day, and had immediately thought, *Crap. There's so many people, it's not going to be a good surf session. Everyone will be cutting me off...* As he paddled out, he noticed the surfers were aggressive, just as he'd expected. In that moment, Troy created a space between a pattern in his thinking and responding, and he paused. In that pause, he reminded himself why he was there that day—he had chosen to be in the water and to surf because he loves it. Rather than filling himself with frustration while trying to catch every wave, he chose to enjoy the ocean and the beautiful day. As waves approached, he hung back and waved people on to take the ride instead of him. He told me he had one of the best surf sessions ever that day. He caught a few waves and had a great time, but, even more important, he felt liberated. He chose joy and happiness.

Viktor Frankl inspires us: choice gives us personal growth and a feeling of liberation. Create space in those moments of your life when you're in a pattern of reacting. If we can pull ourselves out of this loop by creating a small space in the mind, we can **pause and choose our thoughts and actions**. We can cultivate more joy, more compassion, more happiness in our lives. **We always have the power to choose.**

Reflection:
Today, look for opportunities to pause and choose.

At the end of the day, write down any successful pauses.

If you didn't have successful pauses today, take one situation or conversation from the day that could've gone differently. Rewrite it with your own pause and choose scenario to consider a new version of your story.

Practice:
Use your sacred silence during your Golden Practice to stretch and expand your headspace.

Strengthen your ability to pause and choose. Apply this to little moments throughout the day; look for opportunities to change patterns.

DAY 7
Catch a Thought and Flip It

Each of us is responsible for how we see, and how we see determines what we see.

—JOHN O'DONOHUE

So often, we are unaware of how our perspective *(how we see)* determines what we notice in ourselves, others, and the world. Shifting your perspective takes time and practice, and becoming a good observer sets the foundation. It is a skill to become more mind*FUL* and conscious and less mind*LESS* in our perspective, in how we are living. To build this skill, we must strengthen awareness through observation. Observe your thoughts and feelings. Continue to observe, observe, observe. Notice what repeatedly pops up in your mental chatter throughout the day. Identify old patterns of thinking and doing. Become aware of where your mind goes when you are lost in thought. This is an essential step in shifting awareness.

We become better at what we practice, and our minds are the same. When we constantly give attention to thoughts and feelings that don't serve us, those pathways become deeper, stronger, and automatic.

If a dozen balls are coming at you, you must focus your mind and body to move your arms and feet and open your hands to catch the ball. Throughout our days, we have many metaphorical balls bouncing around and grabbing our attention. The trick is to *Catch a Thought*: focus your attention on the ball you want to *catch* in order to *change*. For example, notice yourself going down a habitual path of worry. The first and most important part is to observe your unconscious choice to worry. By catching the worried thought or feeling that doesn't serve you, you create a space in between to choose. Pull your worry in by the tail and observe: *I am worrying (again!)*. Then ask yourself, *Does this serve me*? Now you have a choice.

The mantra "I am too busy" is one I am guilty of repeating. This thought changes *what* and *how* I see throughout my day when I feel like there is not enough time. I realize I don't want to live my life running around feeling unsatisfied due to a sense of time and energy restrictions. I have been practicing catching my words and thoughts. *I am too busy. I don't have enough time.* I am shocked at how often I repeat these thoughts. *Catching* is the first step to *changing*. Through skilled observation and awareness, we offer ourselves a chance to create new pathways in our thinking patterns every time we are able to *Catch a Thought*.

A tandem practice I share with my students and clients is to *Flip It*. We cannot flip or shift a negative thought or situation until we observe, gain awareness, and *Catch It*. Once caught, take a thought or situation and shift the way you see it. Flip it upside down, find a new perspective, try a new approach! Viktor Frankl shares, "When we are no longer able to change a situation, we are challenged to change ourselves." Through finding simple ways to send your thoughts and responses down a different path, *Flipping It* can guide an emotional response, create a physical shift, and turn old, habitual patterns into new ways of seeing and responding.

How *can* we shift our perspectives and patterns out of autopilot? What would that look like?

The Detour

Heading home on my usual route—memorized streets, stoplights, intersections, trees, buildings—I realize I am driving on autopilot. The Jeep seems to drive itself. Then something unexpected catches my eye: a large orange sign, *Road Closed—DETOUR*. All of a sudden, I become focused, alert. The sign reminds me to *catch* myself and be present. Surprisingly, I have to think and navigate the new way home. I notice the trees and flowers I've missed by taking the same path home. After the reroute, I reach my street. Ahh, so grateful for the delight of the new sights and sounds the alternate route gave me.

The New Approach

A client I was working with asked for help in shifting her perspective around challenges in her workplace. After she observed, identified, and *caught* an old, unproductive pattern with a coworker, she chose to change her reaction to the situation. She became calm and, after thinking about it, took a different approach and action. The result: *Flipping It* replaced her irritation with peace and less stress. She shared this *Flip It* experience with her daughter. A few days later, the daughter took her mother's advice and used it in a work situation. *Flipping It* worked for the daughter as well.

FLIP IT is the action of shifting in order to gain a new perspective. You gain a new, creative view of experiences you would have missed through your old pattern of seeing and feeling. Remember, the same type of thinking that created a problem cannot be used to solve it.

If we can *Catch a Thought*, then we can *Flip It*, and
WAKE UP to new opportunities and possibilities.

Reflection:

What patterns are you continually repeating without resolution? Where does your mind go as you move through your day? Notice the messaging in your thoughts and feelings when thinking about different aspects of your life—family, work, health, news... Reflect on how changing the way you respond might change the outcome and create new possibilities. Journal moments throughout your days when you chose to *Catch It and Flip It*.

Practice:

Catch a Thought: Identify one old thought pattern, your own mental mantra, that you would like to change.

Flip It: Stand on your head (literally or figuratively) and see things from a new perspective. Take your habitual mantra and *Flip It*—approach the thought from another angle.

Detour: Go home a different way- change your route. Create your own detour.

DAY 8
Imaginal Cells

Imagination is everything. It is the preview of life's coming attractions. -ALBERT EINSTEIN

As I investigate my milkweed plant, I am excited to find my nine baby caterpillars now fat and almost ready for the next stage of the miraculous metamorphosis of the monarch butterfly. The cute little striped caterpillars will form their chrysalides, at which point nature will get to work transforming these tiny crawlers into majestic winged creatures. The butterfly life cycle is a natural display of the magical and miraculous.

> *Caterpillars represent more than the coming of spring; they symbolize transformation and the possibility of metamorphosis. The caterpillar, a chunky creature close to the earth, literally transforms into a beautiful flying creature. The transformation of the caterpillar is a biological miracle with a message.*
>
> *With my limited knowledge of insects, I always imagined the caterpillar in the cocoon transforming bit by bit, growing wings and butterfly antennae, but the metamorphosis of this creature is, in fact, far more miraculous. Transformation in the insect world, unlike that of mammals, is almost alien or otherworldly. Once in the cocoon, the caterpillar starts to disintegrate into a glob of mush and decay.*
>
> *Unique cells called imaginal cells show up in the butterfly-to-be while it is still a caterpillar. The caterpillar's immune system thinks they are enemies and fights them off. The imaginal cells continue to grow, multiplying like crazy, and eventually take over. Cells start to cluster together into groups that resonate at the same frequency, passing information from one to another. One cluster becomes the wings, another cluster becomes legs, and another the antennae. The research professor Lincoln Brower reports, "And so the transformation of metamorphosis goes... Nothing like this happens in vertebrates—ever. It's a phenomenon of insects and it truly is a miraculous biological process of transformation."*
>
> *What makes imaginal cells truly miraculous is that while within the caterpillar, they were not caterpillar cells, nor were they butterfly cells. They "imagined" themselves! "The term imaginal cell is given to those*

formative, embryonic cells embedded within the caterpillar which imagine and create the butterfly," according to Deanne Bednar, author of "Imaginal Cells: A Metaphor of Transformation."

In Dorien Israel's translation of the 78th Passage of *Tao de Ching*, we read:

> *"The Tao turns the tides and changes caterpillars into butterflies. Do you truly believe that it has less magic, mystery or meaning in store for you?"*

This true story of imaginal cells inspires us to believe in transformation and the power of imagination.

Caterpillars remind us of their message—**What can we imagine for ourselves?**

Reflection:

What are you imagining today? What previews are playing in your mind? Remember, you are the writer. What miracles will you unfold on your Golden Journey?

Call to Action:

Save the endangered monarch butterflies! The western monarchs have had a 99 percent decline in population since the 1980s due to pesticides and loss of habitat. Buy and plant milkweed because raising a caterpillar is rescuing a butterfly.

DAY 9

Travel Light • Feng Shui 風水

He who would travel happily must travel light.
— ANTOINE DE SAINT-EXUPÉRY

Feng shui originated in China almost six thousand years ago. Its literal translation is "wind-water," and it is the study and understanding of energy (qi). It is an ancient method used to optimize space in homes and businesses to bring happiness, abundance, and harmony. Feng shui views architecture in terms of "invisible forces," known as qi, that bind the universe, earth, and humanity together. It is the placement of objects in relation to the flow of qi (氣, "natural energy").

The principle is the same for the spaces you occupy. I describe them as boxes. To understand your living room, you have to look at the bigger container of your house and your neighborhood. Feng shui experts use the old lo pan compass (the oldest compass) to read this space as it pertains to the larger container of the stars and planets. It's fascinating to understand how energy works in space. When we have too many things occupying one space, or things that aren't being utilized, this creates a blockage of energy flow. Feng shui practitioners refer to this as clutter. A simple technique in this tradition is often referred to as clutter clearing.

One of my favorite books on this topic is *Clear Your Clutter with Feng Shui* by Karen Kingston. She describes and maps out how to clear clutter and understand how unused items block the flow of qi in your space. In this system, clearing clutter is one aspect of organizing space to create energy flow. Understanding space is a reflection of specific aspects of our lives. By clearing and shifting physical items, we are able to create a flow in different areas of our lives:

Prosperity	**Reputation**	**Love**
Family	**Health**	**Creativity**
Wisdom	**Career**	**Friendships**

There are so many practical and emotional reasons that we hold on to things. *It was expensive... I might need it in the future... Someone I love gave it to me...* When we let go of things and remove clutter, we open up space for new energy in these aspects of our lives.

In Marie Kondo's method of clutter clearing, she describes the importance of keeping only what brings us joy, surrounding ourselves with the things we love. This is a powerful practice of evaluating things around us that either block energy or create a flow. When considering letting go of something, I am reminded of the time I shared my unused and unloved clothes with two sisters who worked next door. For the following year, I saw shirts, pants, and sweaters being beautifully worn and appreciated, bringing two people joy instead of sitting in my closet. Now, even when I can't see the recipients, I know that when I give things away, someone is using them. It brings me such joy.

Over the years, numerous students have shared their clutter-clearing success stories—people who felt stuck in creativity, wanted to increase wealth, get pregnant... Their stories inspire me. I have witnessed shifts and openings in different aspects of their lives through the practice of letting go and clearing. This process of releasing invites lightness, happiness, and new beginnings. It always gives back. Clearing your unloved, unused clutter is one of the most liberating and powerful practices.

When we begin to implement this in our lives—the practice of observing space as having a flow of energy, seeing how it reflects in your life, skillfully letting go of things—we begin to feel lighter in our emotions, liberated. The more we practice clearing clutter, the better we become at seeing where we can let go of things that no longer serve us.

As a metaphor for how this practice applies to your life's journey, imagine packing for a long hike. You would not pack heavy items you won't need or use. You would pack efficiently, carrying only things useful and loved. What a beautiful image for reflecting on what we carry during our lives' journeys. I invite you to practice letting go and Traveling Light!

Practice:

Choose one space (kitchen, living room, office, bedroom) and choose one area of this space (filing cabinet, closet, bookshelves) to begin your clutter-clearing practice. Identify unused and unloved things that are creating blockages. Package them up and give them away. To continue this practice, follow the method of Karen Kingston or Marie Kondo.

Reflection:

Notice how you feel after giving away something you had kept for a long time or felt you might need in the future, or something that was expensive. Go through parts of your home and see where you could create more flow.

For Your Library:

Clear Your Clutter with Feng Shui by Karen Kingston

The Life-Changing Magic of Tidying Up by Marie Kondo

DAY 10

I Make My Path

The big question is whether you are going to be able to say a hearty yes to your adventure.

— JOSEPH CAMPBELL

Will you say a hearty YES to your next adventure? Joseph Campbell's *The Hero's Journey* inspires us. We relate to the hero because we see ourselves, our stories of love, romance, scary monsters, mystery, and challenges... We live out many adventures in a lifetime—the trick is to see the opportunity in the situations we face. We can begin to see ourselves as the star of each adventure. Will we confidently say yes, knowing we determine our fate?

> On my long plane ride to India, one of the many movies I watched was *Alice in Wonderland*. Well into her adventure, Alice tells one of the characters of her plans to return to the Queen's palace to rescue the Mad Hatter. The hound dog, surprised by her decision (as this was not how the story was foretold), begins to warn, "If you diverge from the path...," to which Alice responds with confidence, "I make the path!"
>
> Barely into my India adventure, I took a divergence from my path. A car accident was not how I anticipated the adventure would unfold. Apparently, none of my trips to India would be complete without a stay at the Columbia Asia Hospital in Mysore. There in the hospital, the adventure unfolded. Nothing was as I had planned.
>
> A severe neck injury left me unable to attend the teachers' training—the reason for my month-long stay in India—and unable to return home. Branching off from the path I envisioned, I set a new course. I created a makeshift rehab center for myself in my small apartment in a rural town in South India. My month of study instead became a time to strengthen and rehabilitate my neck in order to safely return home. It also became an opportunity to reevaluate my life. Two months before the trip to India, my nineteen-year marriage had unexpectedly come to an end. The divorce and car crash, both of which blindsided me, changed my

life. These unforeseen turns forced me to pause and take time to reflect and redirect my life. Like Alice, I wrote my own adventure.

Our stories can be categorized as dramas, romances, comedies, and mystery novels. Even when we think we know how the story will unfold, our lives may surprise us and turn out to be scary, perhaps exciting, mysteries. If you had told me three months before the accident that I would be recreating my life, I would have laughed. My life story became a mystery that led to unexpected twists and turns. Although it was a challenging time, it gave me the opportunity to dig deep to find my strength and faith. Now, when I look back, I see this time as one of the most significant periods of my life. I chose my path. I returned home from India feeling strong and grateful to be alive in a way I'd never experienced before.

A friend asked me, "If you could do it over, what would you change?" I thought, Would I have chosen an easier, less painful version of that chapter of my life? I invite you to reflect on some of the chapters of your story. *Would you have chosen an easier path*? Step back and consider the bigger story of *you*. Identify yourself as the hero. As you turn this page of your life story, choose your own way. Make your own path. Say YES—a big, hearty YES—to your life's adventure.

Reflection:

How does your favorite hero movie inspire your life's journey? Identify chapters of your life as comedy, drama, mystery, or unexpected romance.

Look at the bigger story of your life. Map out the chapters of your life history. What twists and turns and unexpected roads brought you to where you are today? How have you made your own path?

Practice:

Watch your favorite inspiring hero movie tonight, whether true or a fiction favorite—*Out of Africa, Rocky, The Lord of the Rings, The Wizard of Oz*...

DAY 11
Move the Furniture

If you want something you've never had
You must be willing to do something you've never done.
  - attributed to THOMAS JEFFERSON

My life-coaching clients reach out to me when they know they need to shift or change. It's not always a call for help with a problem; sometimes it's a request to reawaken from a feeling of stagnation or being stuck. One of my favorite fun practices to inspire my clients is to ask them to *Move the Furniture.*

Personally, no matter how old I am, no matter where I am on my path, I hope to always be a student of life. I want to continue to change—to reach for more happiness, more joy. I want to feel awe, to be silly, and to grow in wisdom and strength. When I am feeling bored or stuck in any way, *I Move My Furniture.* If I feel flat and uninspired in my teachings, I move the books around on my shelves or put my computer in a different space. I pick flowers and place them around the house. I rearrange a couch or chair and shift what my eyes are used to seeing and the way I walk through my home, office, and yard. Changing furniture forces me to walk differently through my space. These small changes awaken my muse and ignite my creativity!

Moving art and plants, adding flowers: a small change can shift our eyes to look again, to see new possibilities. We unconsciously cycle through patterns of thinking and feeling, but this simple practice wakes us up and switches off autopilot mode. Notice the paths you take as you move through your home, then make a change and mix it up! Shake up old patterns. Move things around to open up your creativity. Gain a new perspective!

Change your external world to recharge and
awaken your internal landscape.

Practice:

Move your desk. Turn your coffee table sideways, move all your files to the other side of your office cabinet, shift your plants to new locations, put your favorite chair in another room, move your photos and art. Be creative!

Reflection:

Observe how you feel when you *Move the Furniture*. Notice how your daily patterns of seeing, doing, and being shift.

DAY 12
Peace Out

When we define symptoms, we think of dysfunction, disorder, depression, anxiety, or heart disease. Within her poem "Symptoms of Inner Peace™," Saskia Davis created a list of symptoms to instead define a state of peace.

"Signs and Symptoms of Inner Peace"
By Saskia Davis © 1984
Excerpted from SYMPTOMS OF INNER PEACE

A tendency to think and act spontaneously rather than on fears based on past experiences

An unmistakable ability to enjoy each moment

A loss of interest in judging other people

A loss of interest in judging self

A loss of interest in interpreting the actions of others

A loss of interest in conflict

A loss of ability to worry

Frequent, overwhelming episodes of appreciation

Contented feelings of connectedness with others & nature

Frequent attacks of smiling

An increasing tendency to let things happen rather than make them happen

An increased susceptibility to love extended by others and the uncontrollable urge to extend it.

Spontaneity, frequent smiling, loss of ability to worry... These are indicators of living in peace. We lose interest in judgment or conflict because we no longer waste energy dwelling on negativity.

Have you ever noticed someone who is tranquil and at peace

YOUR GOLDEN JOURNEY
A 45-DAY PILGRIMAGE TO PERSONAL TRANSFORMATION

and thought, *Why? What is their secret*? Why are they so happy, not stressed? We notice people who are smiling, kind, and joyful, at ease with life and its challenges. Perhaps you think, *What can I do to have more calm, ease, and peace*? For starters, worry less, judge less, and choose to see our connectedness, choose to love. Reread "Signs and Symptoms of Inner Peace" and let these words of wisdom inspire and motivate you.

When we feel connected to nature and to people, we feel more joy. Our time is spent wisely, and happiness, increased energy, peace, and serenity are our reward.

I have been teaching meditation, gratitude, breath, and yoga for over twenty-five years. These are practices that help us create a calm space where we choose our perspective and the lens with which we want to see and live. Like any practice, it's in the doing *and the continuing to do*. If we stop training muscles, it doesn't take long for atrophy to begin. Training consistently keeps the heart, lungs, and legs in shape. It is the same for choosing peace. I believe it's something we need to practice and *continue to practice*. The more we do so, the better we are at showing up and living in peace and happiness.

Practice:

Make a copy of "Signs and Symptoms Inner of Peace" and tape it to your computer or medicine cabinet as a reminder of what peace looks and feels like.

Use your Golden Practice meditation and reflection to increase your inner observations about situations where you can choose peace throughout your day.

Reflection:

What are *your* symptoms of inner peace? Singing? Being silly? Sleeping well and waking up with energy? Smiling? Being kind to others and yourself?

Create a personal list of your "Signs and Symptoms of Inner Peace."

Poster available at: http://www.symptomsofinnerpeace.net/Home.htm

DAY 13
Artist In You

Life is a living canvas.

— DORIEN ISRAEL

You are the artist of the story of your life. There are over seven billion people on the planet, and there have been over a hundred billion to date. With no two people alike, you are one in a hundred billion. You are completely, uniquely you. Everything you do is an expression of you. The way you speak, dress, decorate your home, walk... Your scarf and the way you wear it. The art on your walls, dishes in your cupboard, your furniture—all are reflections of your unique design.

The world is forever static, precise, dependable, predictable, fixed and logical. You, however, are radiant, imaginative, expressive, impetuous, totally alive, undulating, creative energy. You are the cause and the world is your effect.

— Dorien Israel

I invite you to look through the lens of the artist. Do you live a creative life or feel stuck in fixed or logical habitual patterns? How do you show up for your work, respond to problems, talk with friends, cook meals? Create change in the details of your life; express your uniqueness.

The purpose of art is washing the dust of daily life off our souls.

— Pablo Picasso

The ARTIST IN YOU is the way you show up for life.
Like Michelangelo, Picasso, and Rodin, we paint and sculpt our days with our creative flair for living.

Practices: **Wake Up Creative Energies**

- Even though I would not consider myself a painter, when I need to wake up my energy and creativity, I get out a canvas and paint—just fun expressions of colors and images, textures and light. If I like the result, I hang it somewhere for a while. When I feel like doing so, I paint something entirely different over it.
- Take a trip to your local art supply store. Pick up some colored pencils for your journal and maybe even some paints and a canvas.

Reflection:

What are the things that you feel express your extraordinary qualities?
> Write them down.
> Refer to yourself as an artist.
> Use your journal as a space to begin adding color and creativity.

DAY 14
I Am the Master

I am the master of my fate:
I am the captain of my soul.

— WILLIAM ERNEST HENLEY

Some days, I don't feel like the captain of my life ship; instead, I feel like the overworked engine propelling the ship from below. How many things do we try to accomplish in one day? Our modern-day lives, schedules, and pace keep us running, constantly on the go. We are all *aware* of the need to slow down. What keeps us from making the days less crowded, with fewer chores, appointments, and activities?

Perhaps we start with the decision to live more simply. Begin by making conscious decisions to change the pattern. Choose to slow down—walk instead of run through your day. I'll be the first to admit I'm guilty of packing the hours of my days. On my busiest weeks, I feel tired—life is running me rather than me directing my course.

In my studies of Japanese philosophy, I came across the translation of the word *shugyo* in Beth Kempton's book *Wabi Sabi*. *Shugyo* is translated as "training for intuitive wisdom." In the Japanese value system, *the way things are done outweighs what is done*.

Intuitive wisdom is a beautiful way to observe the things we do in terms of value. What has value to you? What is worth your precious moments? How well will you complete a task? It's not about getting a list of twenty things accomplished—*consider how well you did each thing*.

Observe:

- Are you texting and eating?
  - Watching news while eating?
  - (Very bad for your digestion)
  - Driving and eating? (Very dangerous)
- Try sitting down and just eating. Enjoy your food- the taste, the aroma.
- Eat slowly and mindfully. You can always add good company.

> Slow down and live mindfully.
> Nourish your mental, physical and emotional health.

Reflection:

What is worth spending your time doing? Do it with full intention, and do it well. While having coffee with a friend, do you look at your phone, take a call, feel rushed, think about what is next on the agenda? Are you talking on the phone while watering the plants? What would it feel like to simply enjoy being outside, hearing the birds, observing growth or the change in seasons reflected in your yard?

Practice:

Choose fewer activities *but pay greater attention*. Place value on your choices.

Take a few deep, long, slow breaths, and repeat your mantra: I am the master of my fate. *I am the captain of my soul. This is how I choose to live today.*

DAY 15
Choose a Happy Mind

Most folks are about as happy as they make up their minds to be.

—attributed to ABRAHAM LINCOLN

The cover is tattered, worn, taped, and frayed: a sign of a loved book in my library. I read and underlined a great portion of *The Happiness Advantage* by Shawn Achor. I used my underlined pages and notes to create inspiring teachings about the science of happiness, citing new research and studies on neuroplasticity. All the studies and innovative research support our sixteenth president's words of wisdom. We are as happy as we make up our minds to be. It *is* a choice.

This is an old truth, and the words attributed to Lincoln remind us that there is a choice here—we can *make up our minds* to be emotionally healthier. As you reflect on your own thought patterns in moments of struggle, consider not only the specific thoughts but also the overall quality of the messaging in your head.

One of my favorite stories from *The Happiness Advantage* was when Shawn, at one of his corporate lectures on happiness, had gone outside for some fresh air during a break. A man outside said to him, "What a hot day," and went back inside. A second man came outside, looked at Shawn, and said with a smile on his face, "What a beautiful day."

Same weather, same location. Two different experiences.

Author Carlos Castaneda tells us, "The trick is in what one emphasizes. We either make ourselves miserable, or we make ourselves happy. The amount of work is the same."

What consumes your mental and emotional energy? Beautiful days and moments of appreciation? Challenges that you look forward to solving? Friends you want to meet? Or is it worry, criticism, and complaints? It's the same amount of mental space.

Knowing there is a choice in how much energy and time you

spend on any given thought, what emotions or mental messaging would you choose to fill your *space in between*? Would you want to choose happiness, contentment, joy, fulfillment, compassion, and love? Read that list again. Notice that these are all emotions that are generated from the inside out. Rather than waiting for life to show up and be the way you want it to be, YOU get to choose. Choose happiness.

Reflection

Observe times you were able to catch yourself going down an unhappy path in your mind. How were you able to choose a happier thought? Did you choose gratitude or step back and get a bigger perspective? Write a few examples. Continue to reflect and journal throughout your weeks.

Practice:

Catch a complaint or a worry. *Flip It.*
   It may be hot today, but it may also be beautiful.

For Your Library:

Buy two copies of *The Happiness Advantage* by Shawn Achor, one for your library and one to give to a friend. Choose and give happiness.

DAY 16
Energy Banking

Everything is energy and that's all there is to it. Match the frequency of reality you want and you cannot help but get that reality. It can be no other way. This is not philosophy, this is physics.

—attributed to Albert Einstein

Everything that exists is energy. **Energy is all around us—we ARE energy.** Like the air we breathe, this vital life force is invisible to the naked eye. Because we are unable to see energy, we work harder to connect to it. Life force is acknowledged in every culture; it's *qi* or *chi* in China, *prana* in India, *mana* in Polynesia, *nguvu* in West Africa, *aura* in Russia, and *Holy Spirit* in the Western world.

Animals pick up on and read energy. My dog can read the energy of a new person and know whether to trust or be on guard. We, too, have this natural skill—we can identify and tap into our energy and the energy around us. Though this life force is invisible, we can use our ability to read and understand energy to create greater physical and mental health.

I like to use the example of our modern devices—smartphones, tablets, computers. They are powered by an invisible energy source. If the battery is low, it will soon be empty, and the device will no longer work. The smart devices warn us with a notification of *low battery* and flash a red battery icon. We, too, run off energy and may feel vibrant and active or sluggish and depleted. Once we notice *our* energy tank is low, we realize the need to rest, to get more sleep, to move and do something to recharge our battery.

Sleep, exercise, and eating right fuels our energy. We are also fueled by experiences, feelings and situations. You may wake up and take a short walk in nature before you start work, knowing that this will increase your energy. Or you may start your day consumed with worry, checking emails or watching the news, and end up depleting your energy. There are times when you may have started the day with a full tank, battery charged; then something happened to drain that energy. Someone or something zapped your energy.

> *How we fuel our body fuels our spirit and what drains our body, drains our spirit.*
>
> — Caroline Myss

In her books and videos, Myss describes **energy banking**. Observe the people and situations throughout your day that either give you energy or drain your battery. Myss encourages us to become better at reading energy, thus making better energy decisions. Become better at observing what drains or fuels you. Make energy choices that serve you. Shifting out of energy-draining patterns and increasing your good energy investments is a practice and a daily discipline.

Practice:

Observe your energy during your Golden Practice.

Use your ten breaths to calm your energy and fill your tank.

Reflection:

Make a list of the things, people, and situations that drain your energy.

Then make a list of the things, people, and situations that recharge you and fill your energy level.

Replace one energy drain with something or someone that recharges you each day.

DAY 17
Get Up and Move

Excessive sitting has been linked to more than two dozen chronic diseases and conditions including cardiovascular disease, diabetes mellitus, obesity, hypertension, hyperlipidemia, back pain, ankle swelling, and deep vein thrombosis... Studies, thousands of them, drill down to the same point: sitting is lethal.

-DR. DAVID LEVINE, professor of medicine at the Mayo Clinic

Over the years, I have worked with many people who suffer from chronic back pain. I teach yoga and specific stretches and encourage daily walking, but my number one health tip for back pain is MOVE. Get up out of the chair every twenty minutes. I practice what I preach; I do my computer work, texting, and emails at my kitchen counter and standing desk, with frequent breaks for movement. Recently, I didn't take my own advice and spent a few hours sitting. My lower back was in pain for days, a reminder of the critical nature of frequent movement. Get up and move! It's a simple mantra, but it requires us to break old patterns of working and create new methods to be active throughout our days.

The Mayo Clinic published a finding that the third most common cause for doctor visits is back pain, but less than a third of people with back problems consult a physician. This suggests that there is an epidemic of back pain in the United States. We were designed to move, run, walk, climb, skip, and jump. Our modern-day living is modern-day sitting. We wake up, sit for breakfast, sit in our cars, sit at work, get home, sit to eat, and then relax on the couch. We go to a gym or run for exercise for thirty to sixty minutes to offset the other thirteen hours of being in a seated posture.

New data shows that as little as one or two hours of uninterrupted sitting can affect how you process your blood sugar, and can increase risk of cancer, diabetes, and cardiovascular disease, even if you exercise regularly.

—Dr. Joan Vernikos, former director of
NASA's Life Sciences Program

Research shows that though exercise is good for you, it doesn't negate the damage done by extended periods of sitting. Dr. Levine estimates that in the US, we're spending more than half of our waking hours sitting down, either watching TV, driving, or sitting at a desk at work or home.

Standing for prolonged periods can also lead to back problems.

Alan Hedge, professor of ergonomics at Cornell University, recommends sitting twenty out of every thirty minutes at work, standing for eight minutes, and moving around for at least two minutes. Try out the 20-8-2 breakdown; use the timer app on your phone or computer or a kitchen timer. Hedge reminds us to keep in mind that "these numbers are not absolute, it's a guideline."

The Greek philosopher Socrates used two words as a directive for our self-observation: *know thyself*. We observe our old thought patterns in order to shift and change. We read our energy to make better energy-banking decisions. It is equally important to know your own body, to know its limitations. Our miraculous body is constantly communicating with us, and pain indicates a problem. Listen to your body and know thyself. Make shifts that will keep your physical body vibrantly healthy.

MOVE **your way to better health.**

Reflection:

Observe your activity throughout the day. How much time do you spend in a chair? Brainstorm ideas for how to add more movement in your day.

Practice:

Create or buy a standing desk.

Set a timer to get up from your chair every twenty to thirty minutes.

Walk around the house or office. Get a drink of water.

Make a call while standing.

Stand behind a chair and stretch your arms over your head. Clasp your hands behind your back and stretch your shoulders while standing.

Take a five-minute walk during work breaks.

Watch:

Sitting Disease with James Levine, M.D., Ph.D, professor of medicine at Mayo Clinic on www.DianaChristinson.com

DAY 18
Give A Smile

Go through the day as if you were the Dalai Lama undercover.

—JACK KORNFIELD

On my travels to India, I often visit the Tibetan settlement in Bylakuppe. During one of my trips, while shopping at a small handicraft shop, I had a chance encounter with a Tibetan monk named Chusang Rinpoche. He asked my name and where I lived, and when I said California, he smiled and replied, "I am going to California in two weeks." I was thinking, *That's nice; I wonder if he realizes how large the state of California is*. He handed me a card with his name, phone number, and an address in Irvine, California, which just happens to be thirty minutes from my home. I was speechless—What are the chances? My new acquaintance, Chusang, was going to visit a friend who started a foundation to raise money for the monasteries.

This serendipitous encounter fourteen years ago led to a lifelong friendship. He comes to the States from his home in Nepal every few years and always comes to California to visit. On these visits, we walk at the harbor, visit gardens, and go to local restaurants. Chusang always, always greets every person he passes with a smile, a wave, and a warm hello. *He is a walking parade*! The response is typically shock, then a smile and a wave returned. I remember one time we were walking at the harbor, Chusang Rinpoche in his Tibetan robes of deep maroon and gold, and people would wave back at him and stare. Chusang asked, "Do you think they are afraid of me?" I laughed and replied, "No, they are wondering if they just waved at the Dalai Lama!" (as he indeed resembles a younger version of that spiritual leader). We laughed.

Chusang's smile is contagious. He makes friends wherever his path leads. Saying hello is the beginning; then his inquisitive nature draws him to learn more than a name. He leaves his new acquaintances knowing they have made a new friend. I think of Chusang Rinpoche—a monk, a friend—and the simple joy he shares with his smile: a gift to me and anyone open to his warm greeting. It brings me joy to follow his example and smile at strangers and sometimes wave. I love to see a stranger take a second look to see if they recognize me. I hope it brings a smile to their face and a spark of joy.

Thich Nhat Hanh wrote, "Happiness is available. Please help yourself to it." Help yourself to it, and share it. Sprinkle your workplace, neighborhood, drives, and shopping trips with smiles and waves. Add a hello. Join the movement to make the world happier one smile at a time.

Reflection:

Do you remember the last time a smile made your day? Reflect on moments you remember smiling at someone, perhaps a stranger, and getting a smile back in return. How did it make you feel?

Practice:

Share a smile. Try it today! Let it be a gift—for you, the giver, as well as for the receiver.

The Venerable Shiri Chusang Rinpoche is a Tibetan Buddhist monk in the Dalai Lama school of Buddhism. He was named in 1965 by His Holiness the Dalai Lama. Chusang spent seven years under the Dalai Lama's guidance before studying at a monastic university for thirteen years to obtain the traditional degree (equivalent to a doctorate) in 1990. He currently cares for four monasteries in Nepal and India. Read more at DharmaFellowship.org.

DAY 19
Nature's Medicine

To the body and mind... cramped by noxious work or company, nature is medicinal and restores their tone. The tradesman, the attorney, comes out of the din and draft of the street and sees the sky and the woods and is a man again. In their eternal calm, he finds himself. The health of the eye demands a horizon. We are never so tired so long as we see far enough

-RALPH WALDO EMERSON

When was the last time you felt weary or depressed, went outside for a walk, and felt noticeably better? Humans were meant to interact with nature, as we are indeed a part of nature. The trees clean the air we breathe, the sun keeps us warm and provides vitamin D, the earth releases essential negative ions. Spending time in nature provides protection against a startling range of diseases, including depression, diabetes, obesity, ADHD, cardiovascular disease, and cancer. By living in union with nature, we benefit from its healing properties through daily doses of this powerful medicine.

According to the Environmental Protection Agency, the average American spends 93 percent of their life indoors: 87 percent of their life is inside buildings, then another 6 percent of their life is in automobiles. That leaves only 7 percent of their entire life spent outdoors. That's only one-half of one day per week out in nature.

Shocking? How much time do you spend in nature? Count from the time you wake up, eat, work, play, work out, go to bed. What percentage of time were you outside in nature, among trees and flowers or near a stream or lake? Do the math and calculate how much time you spend outdoors, connecting with nature. We have been civilized and comforted into weakening our bodies, immune systems, and minds, disconnected from nature. Nature is medicine; we need more of it.

Your Nature's Medicine Prescription:

- Daily dose of time outside
- Have your morning tea or coffee outside
- Sacred silence and journal under a tree
- Lunch or lunch break walk outside
- Evening walk through your neighborhood
- Weekly long hike in a local park or forest

Practice:

Take time each day to walk and sit outside. Get out of your home, office, or car, and get back into nature. **Increase the amount of time you spend outside**, and invite your friends and family to join you.

Reflection:

Reflect on how you feel when you take your dose of *nature's medicine.*

DAY 20
Forest Bathing

Thousands of tired, nerve-shaken, over-civilized people are beginning to find out going to the mountains is going home; that wilderness is a necessity... —JOHN MUIR

After a long day, I go outside to rest and sit on my wooden bench. The sun has set; the subtle colors of dusk bring this day to a gradual end; I hear the sounds of nature settling and preparing for sleep. I am enjoying this peaceful time, listening to the gentle breeze, the branches and leaves in the wind. The thin slice of silver moon beyond the pine branch looks like it was framed, a magnificent painting in front of me. I slow down and connect with nature's beauty in my surroundings; this is medicine for my body, energy, and spirit. Bathing in my personal forest, I am nourishing my soul.

The immunologist Dr. Qing Li came to Japan in the 1980s to study medicine. During the course of his medical research, he became interested in the health benefits of time spent in nature. His work revealed that connecting to nature would benefit everyone, especially members of the Japanese workforce who were literally working themselves to death. In Japan, the word karoshi means "death from overwork." Stress levels were causing heart disease, strokes, and death. Dr. Qing Li has devoted thirty years of studies to the prescription for this: shinrin-yoku, or forest bathing. In his years of research, he found that spending mindful time in the forest or in nature can restore a sense of balance—a sense of wonder, of beauty and calm. It can be medicine: a prescription for a healthier, happier life.

The key to unlocking the power of the forest is in the five senses. Let nature enter through your ears, eyes, nose, mouth, hands and feet. Listen to the birds singing and the breeze rustling in the leaves of the trees. Look at the different greens of the trees and the sunlight filtering through the branches. Smell the fragrance of the forest and breathe in the natural aromatherapy of

> *phytoncides. Taste the freshness of the air as you take deep breaths. Place your hands on the trunk of a tree. Dip your fingers or toes in a stream. Lie on the ground. Drink in the flavor of the forest and release your sense of joy and calm. This is your sixth sense, a state of mind. Now you have connected with nature. You have crossed the bridge to happiness.*
>
> —Dr. Qing Li, "The Benefits of Forest Bathing" (*Time* magazine)

Forest Bathing Medicine:

Spending ten minutes daily in nature is medicine for body, mind, and spirit.

- Boosts immune system functioning—increases amount of body's natural killers (NK) cells
- Improves mood
- Increases energy levels
- Improves sleep
- Increases ability to focus, even in children with ADHD
- Accelerates recovery from surgery or illness
- Reduces blood pressure

From Dr. Qing Li's short video "The Art and Science of Forest Bathing with Dr Qing Li"

Unplug; leave your box. Nature is calling: a green lush tree, leaves in the wind, songs of the birds, smells of the season—nature's medicine awaits you.

T. S. Eliot wrote, "We had the experience but missed the meaning."

Do not miss the meaning or the medicine.

Practice:

A daily forest bath.

Go out in nature with intention. Tap into your senses, smell the grass and pine trees, feel the warmth of the sun, hear the wind and leaves in the trees, see the vibrant colors, walk slowly or sit. Take it in.

Don't take your stress with you. Leave your phone at home or turn it off. Instead of using your devices to count steps or check on heart rate, unplug. Let the forest bathe you with peace.

Reflection:
Write in your journal or meditate on how you felt when you spent time in nature, forest bathing with your five senses. Reflect and describe how your senses were awakened through your forest bath.

For Your Library:
Into the Forest: How Trees Can Help You Find Health and Happiness by Dr. Qing Li

Watch:
Dr. Qing Li's short video: *The Art and Science of Forest Bathing with Dr Qing Li* at www.DianaChristinson.com

DAY 21
Barn's Burnt Down

Barn's burnt down—
Now
I can see the moon.

— MIZUTA MASAHIDE

The relationship that you vowed would last forever abruptly ends. The job no longer exists. The home is lost in a wildfire. The diagnosis you never thought you'd hear. Life changes with little or no warning. *Barn's burnt down*—a metaphor for loss.

This thought-provoking haiku was written in the seventeenth century by Japanese poet and samurai Mizuta Masahide. After over three hundred years, these nine words are still powerful and evocative.

Now I can see the moon. A metaphor not only for a new beginning but for a new beginning that came from loss, perhaps sadness, and letting go. The moon beautifully speaks of opportunity for growth and change.

This timeless and universal Japanese poem reminds me of *The Hero with a Thousand Faces*, written by Joseph Campbell in 1949. Campbell mapped out the hero's journey in stages. The archetypal hero begins his journey and encounters a separation and initiation, embarking on the path to transformative change. In the classic story *The Wizard of Oz*, Dorothy is separated from home and family by a tornado. The storm represents loss and leads to her initiation, her journey to Oz along a golden path that offers challenges, opportunities to learn and grow, as she finds her way home. Dorothy is not the same person she was before the tornado. Now appreciative of her home, family, and friends, she returns with new strength and perspective—a transformed Dorothy.

The burnt barn and the tornado are pieces of *your* hero's story, metaphors for your tragedies, failures, and loss. Your hero's call is to identify the storm and face it with a sense of courage and hope. If you look at your bigger life story, you can see many tornadoes and storms and how they have impacted your growth into the person you are today. Your personal story reminds you of your initiation and adventures to find your way home. Many universal stories, like that of Dorothy in Oz, as well as true stories, are inspiring invitations to view our challenges as opportunities for transformation.

Open your heart and mind to possibilities and opportunities that arise from challenge and loss.

Reflection:

Identify parts of your life when you experienced a separation or loss that brought you to a new place that transformed you. Write down losses that granted you opening or perspective.

Use this as a reminder the next time you feel a loss or a change.

# DAY 22
Lucky Me!

Open your heart to all these blessings, and let them flow through you, that everyone whom you will meet on this day will be blessed by you, just by your eyes, by your smile, by your touch, just by your presence. Let the gratefulness overflow into blessing all around you.

—Benedictine monk BROTHER DAVID STEINDL-RAST

The room is still partially dark, with a dim glow from my candle and the smell of incense. Silence. The only noise is in my busy head. I take a few breaths with awareness and still my mind. I settle into a feeling of peace. I begin my practice of gratitude. With my hands over my heart, I visualize and fill my mind with people, experiences, precious things. My mantra for each: *I am grateful, I am lucky, I am blessed.* Every cell in my body is filled with gratitude.

Messages of Gratitude

I have been practicing and teaching gratitude as a meditation for over a decade. Six years ago, I began a new gratitude practice, asking my students to look around at their lives and consider: Where do you see messages of gratitude? In your mailbox, in simple social acts and exchanges, in meditation or prayers, in celebrations? Also consider the more obvious gratitude messaging we see everywhere—bags, shirts, wall art?

"The message of gratitude is everywhere." I had recently noticed that my jeans came with a message on the fly—*Lucky You*—and I shared, "Even our jeans are reminding us to be grateful!" Once the group stopped giggling, I invited my students to each put a note in their pants pocket that says *Lucky Me!* I added, "Get a stack of sticky notes and fill out an entire pad with *Lucky Me!* Post them everywhere. On your computer, in your wallet, on the bathroom mirror, in a drawer, on the fridge, in a jacket pocket, with some hidden in places you will find later. The notes will serve as a reminder to pause, smile, and be grateful as you move through your days."

Lucky Me has become a meaningful mantra for myself and our community. After years of teaching this practice, it has become part of the vocabulary at the yoga school and among friends. We text each other ending with *Lucky Me*! We end a phone call with, "I love you, lucky me!" Every day, I see notes my students have hung around our yoga room stuck next to pictures and light switches. Sometimes I come across one that has been hidden, and I always smile when I see those words: *Lucky Me*. I am reminded that language is powerful—just two simple words can change our thinking and feeling.

How often will you say *lucky me* today?

When Feeling Unlucky:

Gratitude is a practice. It works when we are feeling great but is also powerful when we are able to use it as a way to shift out of a challenging experience or a negative feeling or pattern. A *Lucky Me* mindset is not about rose-colored glasses or denial, though I often get the expected pushback: "Life is hard and unfair. We're not always lucky and blessed." Recently, my teeth hurt, and I needed a root canal, something you cannot deny is unfortunate. After experiencing that initial unlucky feeling, I shifted: I have a great dentist and insurance, and I am able to pay for the procedure. *Lucky me!* I invite you to honor what is hard and then shift from that place to something real that gives you the opportunity to be positive.

> Create a *pause, a space in between*, and shift your mind's pathways back to happiness with gratitude.

Reflection:

Reflect on five to ten things that you are grateful for. After citing each one individually, recite or write the mantra Lucky Me. Notice how you feel when you add feeling lucky and blessed to your daily gratitude.

Practice:

Get a pad of sticky notes and fill it with Lucky Me! messages. Put them all around your house, office, and car. Hide a few in drawers, pockets, and cupboards.

When you least expect it, you will see a reminder and smile.

Bonus:

Share gratitude! Get a second pad of sticky notes and fill it with Lucky Me! messages for your partners, children, teachers, friends, coworkers. A moment of pause, an extension of gratitude. You can add a line, such as Lucky Me—you are in my life! Be creative, and have fun spreading gratitude, smiles, and love! Let's fill the world with gratitude.

DAY 23
Wild Life

Tell me, what is it you plan to do with your one wild and precious life? - MARY OLIVER

I am a lover of books, words, poetry, and quotes. At a young age, I pretended to work in a library, stacking my parents' books and encyclopedias (a fact that dates me). In high school, I worked in the school library as a proud book hound. My love for books continues, particularly for inspirational books. My home library is filled with books about psychology and philosophy, their pages underlined, highlighted, marked with paper scraps. As a teacher, I pass on my favorite quotes in hopes of inspiring others.

Over the years, there have been a few poems and quotes that literally changed my life: a set of words that not only inspires but becomes a part of how I want to show up and live. One quote by Mary Oliver is a treasured favorite. The quote is a question at the end of the longer poem titled "The Summer's Day."

> *"Tell me, what is it you plan to do with your one wild and precious life?"*

These sixteen words together are a powerful universal question: *What are you going to do with the gift that is your life?*

In one of my teachings, I ask students: *What makes a day great?* I wait and listen to their answers: being with my family, listening to music, watching the sunset, sipping a cup of coffee outside, a visit from a hummingbird... At the end of the day, when you crawl into bed and review the past sixteen hours, will you say *This was a great day*? It's not always the big things, like the day you were married, bought a new house, were promoted. It's the little things—the look of love, the gathering of friends, the spontaneous dancing in the kitchen.

Your days become your weeks; they become your years, your life. One day you will take your last breath. In that moment, will you say *This was a great life*? Will you say *I made the most of my one wild and precious life*?

ONE—because we live this life only once
WILD—because life is meant to be an adventure
PRECIOUS—because our time here is a gift

Practice:

Today, choose two or three things to do or experience that will make you smile and will contribute to this being a great day.

Reflection:

What did you do that made today great?
    What will you do to make tomorrow great?
    Reflect on or write three words—*one, wild*, and *precious*. How do these describe your life?

☀ CONGRATULATIONS!

You are halfway through your journey.

Life can certainly be wild, and this is a loving mid-point reminder from me to you:

Offer yourself compassion and do the best you can as you move through the days. This is your journey, it is meant to serve you, and I want you to enjoy the process. We all get sidetracked, and while you might find yourself missing a day or two, or taking more time with one entry along the way, it's all a beautiful part of your path. Allow the teachings to naturally show up during your days, pay attention to your breath, and enjoy moments of gratitude. If you miss a day of reading and reflection, give yourself permission to let this journey unfold and return to your practice.

Even a drop, a sip, any small inward retreat to fill your cup, to fill your gas tank, will benefit you. Showing up for yourself allows you to elevate the way you show up for others. The destination is your continued practice of making time for yourself to be inspired, connect with nature, and nurture your spirit. This is the true journey and a lifelong destination.

> *Saying that you don't have time to improve your thoughts and your life is like saying you don't have time to stop for gas because you're too busy driving. Eventually it will catch up with you."*
> —Robin Sharma

I lovingly support your journey.
Continue to make time to fill your tank.
Set intentions and be kind to yourself.
Remember, there is no right or wrong way to travel.

Blessings on your journey,
Your Guide, Diana

YOUR GOLDEN JOURNEY
A 45-DAY PILGRIMAGE TO PERSONAL TRANSFORMATION

DAY 24
Giving Bread

Life's most persistent and urgent question is, "What are you doing for others?"

- MARTIN LUTHER KING JR.

A friend shared a story of giving the most uncommon yet precious gift, and it reminded me of one of the simple, moving stories Viktor Frankl shares in *Man's Search for Meaning*. It's a story of kindness from the most unlikely person—one of the prison guards. Frankl was working at a labor camp where the prisoners were malnourished, beaten, and literally worked to death. One day, a guard secretly gave Frankl a small crust of bread that he had rationed from his own breakfast. The gesture of kindness brought Viktor to tears: "It was far more than the small piece of bread which moved me to tears at that time. It was the human 'something' which this man also gave me—the word and look that accompanied the gift."

My friend Sharon lost her husband a number of years ago. He was the love of her life, a carpenter, a woodworker whose tools were an extension of him. To keep memories alive, she kept only a few precious things that belonged to him, including his tools.

Years later, while browsing through postings from nearby contractors online, Sharon noticed a post from a contractor who wrote that a car belonging to one of his workers had been stolen. The car had all the worker's tools in it. He could not afford new tools and was unable to work. She remembered her husband telling the story of his car being broken into and all his tools stolen. He was devastated and also unable to afford new tools. Without hesitation, she listened to her heart and reached out to the contractor to give him the tools that had belonged to her husband. "Please, take whatever you need." Her heart led her to give this man her most cherished belongings. I think of how much this must have meant for the worker to receive and the gesture of true kindness that brought them both a deep joy.

This is a beautiful story of the act of giving. Our giving of bread may be on a smaller level but just as valuable. It could be a kind word—*You look beautiful today. I am grateful you are in my life*. Perhaps a gesture of hope—*I believe in you. You inspire me*. It may be a gift of time, like bringing a friend food when they are hurting. I remember a special gift my friend brought me to cheer me up—a batch of my favorite cookie dough and a bouquet of flowers left at my door.

I often think about the guard in Victor Frankl's story and how it must have brought him some solace in a horrendous time to help one person in a small way.

> **We make a living by what we get, but we make a life by what we give.**
> **—*Winston Churchill***

How do we give bread? What are some simple, hope-filled gestures of kindness? It is at times when we feel we have little for ourselves that we dig into our pockets to find that small something to share with someone in need.

Reflection:

Journal or sit in reflection and think of one to three special gifts you have given that brought you deep joy. Remember receiving a gift that was more than the gift or act itself—one that gave you hope, made you feel loved, and brought you joy.

Practice:

Open your heart to someone. Show kindness, and let your heart lead. When you have an opportunity, show compassion. Reach in your pocket and give the gift of kindness. You don't need to go in search of the right occasion. Open your heart—opportunities for giving will find you.

 DAY 25

A Healthy Mental Diet

A person is limited only by the thoughts that he chooses. - JAMES ALLEN, AS A MAN THINKETH

In the early 1900s, British philosophical writer James Allen was a pioneer in the positive psychology and self-help movement. His philosophy of happiness was based on the power to choose our thoughts in order to create our reality. Allen's book *As a Man Thinketh* is filled with inspiration about the power of our thoughts; his words still ring true today and continue to inspire.

I often consider this concept of the power of choice in regard to how I nourish my physical body. What we consume makes us either healthy or sick. I can choose to eat healthy, natural, fresh, whole foods. My body feels better when I fuel it with healthy foods. I feel light, have more energy, and everything works better. If I choose to eat processed and fast foods, I have less energy, feel stiff, become irritable, and get sick.

I love this inspiration from an extraordinary woman who referred to herself as Peace Pilgrim:

> *I don't eat junk foods and I don't think junk thoughts!*
> *Let me tell you, junk thoughts can destroy you even more quickly than junk food. Junk thoughts are something to be wary of.*

Reaching for that big bag of potato chips, I may stop to consider, Do I really want to feel crappy later? Perhaps this quote is a great reminder of how we may feel after consuming too many negative, unhealthy thoughts.

What happens when we consume negative thoughts throughout our days, for weeks and months on end? The same result: we get sick. We get heart disease, ulcers, high blood pressure.

We care for our mental health in the same way we care for our bodies. My husband's story is a great example. He used to be a three-hundred-pound lineman. Cheeseburgers and fries were regulars on the menu. He lost one hundred pounds and kept them off, transforming into a healthy man who was an inspiration to others. People would always ask, "How did you do it?" His reply was, "First, I stopped having cheese on my burger. Then, I stopped having fries with every meal." He started with *small, simple changes* that made his health and weight loss achievable but sustainable. Use this as your inspiration: What is your mental junk? What are regulars on your menu?

For years, my mental junk food was worry. I realized that the more worry chips I ate, the more I wanted; they're addictive. I made a conscious decision to decrease my worry and replace it with a healthy practice of letting go, a dose of trust. Over the past years, I have literally changed my amount of worry. My friends would agree: it is noticeable. I lost the weight of worry and feel lighter and healthier.

Mental Junk Food: *worrying, gossiping, holding on to anger, criticism, jealousy, pessimism, unkindness, being condescending*

Mental Health Food: *optimism, joy, gratitude, love, hope, kindness, compassion, forgiveness*

You—and only you—are responsible for what you consume. **Make it a healthy choice.**

Practice:

Start small. Identify two junk thoughts from the junk food list or make your own.

Identify two healthy thoughts from the health food list or make your own.

Decrease one or two junk thoughts a day and replace them with healthy ones.

Reflection:

At the end of your day, ask yourself: What thoughts did I consume (*or what consumed me*) throughout this day?

Write down what created negative thoughts in your headspace today and where they were created. Perhaps it's a person or situation at work or an aspect of your relationship that makes you impatient or irritable.

Write down any thought patterns or autopilot reactions you recognized.

Pause and reflect, then *choose* a different thought. Write it down

- *Peace Pilgrim, or Mildred Lisette Norman (1908–1981), was an American spiritual teacher, mystic, pacifist, and vegetarian activist. In 1952, she became the first woman to walk the entire length of the Appalachian Trail in one season. In 1953, Norman set off from the Rose Bowl parade on New Year's Day with a goal of walking the entire country for peace. She left her given name behind and took up a new identity: Peace Pilgrim. Her goal: to walk "coast to coast for peace." She spent twenty-eight years on her journey.*

Read more from, "Peace Pilgrim's 28-Year Walk For 'A Meaningful Way of Life.'" at NPR.org.

DAY 26
Giving a Garland of Gratitude

If the only prayer you ever say in your entire life is thank you, it will be enough.

— MEISTER ECKHART

At parent-teacher conference time, eight-year-old Gwendolyn's teacher shared a story with the child's mother: "Did you know that every single day after class, your daughter thanks me for teaching her? She is the only student who has ever thanked me, and she does it *every single day* before leaving." What joy and pride Gwendolyn's mother, a friend of mine, felt as she told me this story. Her sweet young daughter gave a simple but powerful gift: sincere, heartfelt gratitude. So often it is the young ones that inspire us!

Gwendolyn's story reminds me of a simple ritual of gratitude I began while studying yoga with my teacher in India. Every day after practice, the students would go outside and greet a gentleman who crafted and sold garlands of strung flowers, called *pushpamala*. When a garland was purchased, he would wrap the flowers in a banana leaf and tie it with a thread. Each day, I would purchase a garland of fragrant jasmine for my teacher. I would patiently wait to present my garland of gratitude to him. Even on the busiest days, I never missed the opportunity to perform this ritual of offering thanks. I vividly remember my teacher's happiness and joy in receiving this gesture of appreciation.

In India, the word *guru* means someone or something that brings light to your life's path. This is more than a teacher: the literal translation for the Sanskrit word guru is "dispeller of darkness." We encounter teachers, mentors, guides, and experts who share their light of knowledge and help us grow.

When we reflect on the beauty of Gwendolyn's story, this young girl reminds us of how people and experiences are teachers and bring light to our path.

> **I invite you to extend a garland of gratitude to someone who has shed light on your life's journey.**

Reflection:

Open your heart and mind to the many teachers who have shared their light on your path. Reflect and journal on how they have impacted your life.

Practice:

Gratitude Meditation: Hands over your heart, say thank you for each teacher.

Choose one person who has brought light to your path. Write a note or make a gesture of gratitude. It could be a family member, teacher, friend, neighbor. Receiving the gift of gratitude will make their day, and you will experience the joy of giving.

DAY 27

Bring the Outdoors In

You can't buy happiness but you can buy plants, and that's pretty much the same thing.
—Unknown

The deep, vibrant red of the mandevilla pulls my attention to the window. The green leaves, red flowers, and blue sky are a delight, a gift. I pause to enjoy and notice the sounds of the birds and wind. I am in nature, standing in my kitchen. When we cannot be *out* in nature, we can bring nature's medicine *in*, another *shinrin-yoku* practice for when you can't be outside.

> **From Shinrin-Yoku: The Art and Science of Forest Bathing by Dr. Qing Li**
> **Fill your house with plants**
>
> This might seem obvious, but there are many more reasons to bring plants indoors than simply to make your home look like a forest.
>
> First, they help us to breathe. When we breathe in, we bring oxygen into our bodies. When we breathe out, we release carbon dioxide. Plants do the opposite: they absorb carbon dioxide and release oxygen. So having plants indoor increases the oxygen in our homes—and that is good for us. Oxygen affects every part of our bodies and making sure we get good-quality air is essential to our health.
>
> Most plants switch at night and begin to absorb oxygen and release carbon dioxide, but not all plants do this. Some, like orchids and succulents, also release oxygen at night. These are good plants to fill your bedroom with so that oxygen levels stay high while you sleep. Indoor air can be between two and five times as polluted as the air outdoors, and plants are natural air-purifiers. They act like sponges, soaking up the toxic chemicals found in paints, fabric, cigarettes and cleaning products. As part of a study that looked at ways to clean the air in space stations, NASA came up with a list of the top-ten air-purifying plants:
>
> | | | | |
> |---|---|---|---|
> | Peace lily | Golden pothos | English Ivy | Chrysanthemum |
> | Gerbera daisy | Snake plant | Bamboo palm | Azalea |
> | Red-edge dracaena | | Spider plant | |

When you can't get outside, bring the healing fragrances of nature inside with essential plant oils. Essential oils can be especially beneficial for the immune system due to their antibacterial, antiviral, and antifungal properties. Not only can they aid in fighting off a wide range of pathogens, but they can also stimulate the immune system as well.

THE NINE MOST BENEFICIAL OILS:

| Lavender | Eucalyptus | Oregano | Niaouli | Clove Bud |
| Palmarosa | Peppermint | Tea Tree | Rosemary | |

Bring the live green trees, plants, and flowers into your kitchen, bedroom, office. Open windows; arrange flowers. Use the plant medicine of essential oils, and surround yourself with the healing energy of nature in your *inside* space.

Practice:

Take an indoor forest bath:

- Plant trees and shrubs outside your windows and doors.
- Keep houseplants in your windows and all over the house.
- Keep your windows clean to allow in more sunlight.
- Open your windows to allow fresh air into your home.
- Place photos or artwork depicting natural scenery in your home and workplace.
- Stay in touch with the seasons; notice the changes through your window and in your courtyard.
- Listen to sounds of nature on a music station.
- Place a small fountain in your home or on your patio for the sound of water.
- Burn naturally scented candles or incense, or use an oil diffuser.
- Arrange fresh flowers in vases all around your home and office.
- Be creative and come up with your own unique ways to bring the outdoors in.

Reflection:

How do you feel when you bring nature into your inside spaces? Reflect and journal about how nature's medicine has changed how you felt or perhaps how you responded to a situation in your day. Did your indoor forest bath bring you joy? Did it help you slow down or gain perspective?

# DAY 28

Dancing in the Rain

Joy is in fact our birthright and even more fundamental than happiness. - DALAI LAMA XIV

Children are joyful beings and express their delight through giggles, smiles, and laughter. One of my favorite little friends loves the rain. She gets excited to put on her rainbow shirt and colorful rain boots, runs outside to the biggest puddle, and dances, splashes, giggles, and twirls. She tops it off with both hands up in the air, yelling, *"Yay!"* She is pure *joy!*

Like my young friend, I chose joy at a young age—or perhaps joy chose me. I spent my early years on a small family farm in Michigan. With few families in this rural area, I spent most of my time outside after school and would walk alone in the forest behind our property. It was always an adventure, and I imagined wonderful things as I picked flowers and sang. I filled my mind and time with joy; joy was my mode of being.

As a grown-up, I still like to hike my favorite trails, pick flowers, and sing. I love to twirl my little friend and giggle together as we get dizzy and tumble joyfully to the floor. When was the last time you giggled and sang? As adults, we sometimes put joy in a closet. We wait for the right occasion, as we do with a winter coat or special hat, saving joy for the appropriate situation. But joy, even in the hardest of times, is a gift and powerful medicine. Being a bit silly, laughing, and smiling is contagious. Pay attention—a few days without laughter, smiling, and joy is a detriment to our health.

Happiness is not a station you arrive at, but a manner of traveling.

— Margaret Lee Runbeck

We often think of joy as a response—but joy is a way of traveling. It's a way of seeing the world and experiencing its awe and beauty, even in unexpected moments.

I am reminded of this by young Diana singing in the woods. What brought you joy when you were young? Today, bring joy out of the closet and play. Dance in the rain, sing along to your favorite song, twirl.

Remind yourself that today is an opportunity to travel through your moments, happy and joy filled.

Reflection:

Make a *play*-list of things that brought you joy when you were young. Make a second play-list of activities and things that currently bring you joy. Reflect on what you might bring into your current joy from your past. Journal new ideas to bring joy out of the closet and into your life.

Practice:

Choose from your joy play-list and add one or two things to your daily routine. Mix it up each day. Today, play music while you cook. Tomorrow, turn your lunch break into a picnic. The next day, read your favorite poetry or meet up with a loved one for coffee.

Display Margaret Lee Runbeck's quote "Happiness is not a station you arrive at, but a manner of traveling."

For Your Library:

The Book of Joy: Lasting Happiness in a Changing World by His Holiness the Dalai Lama, Desmond Tutu, and Douglas Carlton Abrams

Read:

For more ideas, visit www.DianaChristinson.com for our readers' playlist of Joy.

The Invitation

So get ready for some new freedom, some dangerous permission, some hope from nowhere, some unexpected happiness, some stumbling stones, some radical grace...

— RICHARD ROHR

I read the poem "The Invitation" by Oriah Mountain Dreamer in college when I was a young, ambitious, curious dreamer. Three decades later, I am still a dreamer. I am a wiser, seasoned adventurer who continues to ask questions and remains curious and excited about life. Oriah wrote "The Invitation" as an expression of her own life, her joys and challenges. The poem was a call to action, using ninety-one lines expressing universal opportunity to look at, change, question, and celebrate life.

Oriah's poem, when used as a guide for self-inquiry, discovery, and changes on our lives' journeys, asks questions of us that can awaken something new as we live the different chapters of our lives. An inspirational and powerful tool to revisit along your hero's journey, "The Invitation" connects you with your true self.

> **Excerpts from "The Invitation" by Oriah Mountain Dreamer**
>
> It doesn't interest me who you know or how you came to be here.
>
> I want to know if you will stand in the center of the fire with me and not shrink back.
>
> It doesn't interest me where or what or with whom you have studied.
>
> I want to know what sustains you from the inside when all else falls away.
>
> I want to know if you can be alone with yourself and if you truly like the company you keep in the empty moments.

Throughout the poem, Oriah asks the reader to consider and ultimately answer questions such as Do you truly know yourself? Do you know your heart's desire? Do you know the desires of people you choose to share in deep friendships and partnerships? Oriah asks, "Can I disappoint another to be true to myself?"

This is a call to practice svadhyaya—to get close to yourself, understand your dreams and feelings, and embrace your authenticity.

Of all the people and subjects you will study in a lifetime, the most important person to get close to is YOU.

Reflection:

Read the poem in its entirety, and handwrite the words in your journal. Underline and highlight the parts most meaningful to you at this time in your life's journey.

Write your own invitation. What questions would you ask? What stirs your soul? What do you dare to dream?

Practice:

Take Oriah's words, or your own, with you on this Golden Journey. Keep them with you for future adventures as you unfold chapters of your "wild and precious" life.

Read the poem again next year and notice which questions speak to you.

Read:

Read and save Oriah Mountain Dreamer's full poem, The Invitation, at www.DianaChristinson.com

DAY 30
Reach for the Sun

The person who risks nothing, does nothing, has nothing. All we know about the future is that it will be different. But perhaps what we fear is that it will be the same. So we must celebrate the changes. Because, as someone once said, "Everything will be all right in the end. And if it's not all right, then trust me: it's not yet the end.
    —The Best Exotic Marigold Hotel

My house is filled with plants; one was gifted by a friend as a special way to remember my husband, Richard, when he passed. Lately, my special plant has been struggling, losing its vibrant colors and leaves. I knew it needed to be repotted, fed, or moved to a new spot. I moved the struggling plant to a space outside my back door, a temporary home until I could buy a new pot and soil. I knew I didn't want to leave it out back for long because there wasn't much sun in that area.

I was busy and forgot about the plant for a few days. One day, I opened the door to leave for work and noticed that the plant, which had been straight a few days earlier, was now sideways, stretching for the back door. Shocked, I stopped. It looked as if it was reaching for me. Setting down my bags, I got up close to the plant to investigate. I realized that it was, in fact, reaching. It was outstretched toward this small sliver of sunlight that fell between my carport and roof. My sickly plant was reaching for the sun, growing and extending to find the light, to survive. It struck me: *what a beautiful message*. A beautiful message for myself at that moment. I, too, had been struggling with personal challenges, what to do and how to do it, how to fix things. The green arms of the plant reaching toward the sun to find the source of light and nourishment had a message for me.

I paused from my rushing and smiled. Thanking the plant, I considered, *What is my sun?* What is my source of nourishment during this dark time in my life? That day, I reached for some quiet time outside, enjoying music and a special dinner. I treated myself to a movie with popcorn and spent time with a dear friend. The next day, I had more energy and felt a hopeful desire to be creative about my challenges. In my own way, I reached for the sun.

One of the many rituals at my yoga school is to give students a simple teaching and an inspirational quote. I make copies of the quotes so the students can take the inspiration with them. Over the years, my students have saved the quotes and shared the special meaning they hold. One of my favorite quotes I shared was from the movie *The Best Exotic Marigold Hotel*, and I remember sharing it during a time when the yoga school was moving and faced with business challenges. (I've also used it as the epigraph for this chapter.) Years after I shared it, my student Bella sent me a picture of a piece of paper that was worn at the folds from being opened and tucked away again over the years. It was a quote she had saved, kept close for so long, that had inspired her during some difficult times of illness, school, moving... You could see how many times Bella had opened and closed it, looking for hope and inspiration.

As *The Best Exotic Marigold Hotel* tells us, if it's not all right, it's not over—things may shift and change in ways we could not possibly imagine today. There is hope in these words and hope found in a struggling plant extended out toward the sun.

Celebrate unexpected changes. Be optimistic about your future. Stay open to what's possible. Find your nourishment and *Reach for the Sun*.

Reflection:

Copy or handwrite the Best Exotic Marigold Hotel quote in your journal or in a place to remind you that the path ahead is yours to create.

What is your sun? What nourishes you?

Make a list.

Hikes in nature   Watching butterflies   Gardening   Walking the dogs

Practice:

Choose one or two items from your list and add them to your daily routine.

DAY 31
Wabi-Sabi

Put simply, wabi sabi gives you permission to be yourself. It encourages you to do your best but not make yourself ill in pursuit of an unattainable goal of perfection. It gently motions you to relax, slow down and enjoy your life. And it shows you that beauty can be found in the most unlikely of places, making every day a doorway to delight.
—Beth Kempton

I first connected to this sense of beauty while living in Japan, where I developed an appreciation for the country's art, culture, and philosophy. Drawn to Zen aesthetics and a minimalist lifestyle and finding beauty in nature and simplicity, I first learned of *wabi-sabi* while studying Japanese philosophy.

> *Wabi-sabi is a beauty of things imperfect, impermanent, and incomplete. It is a beauty of things modest and humble.*
> — Leonard Koren

The *wabi-sabi* philosophy is a way of living, one that honors the *slow and mindful, simple and minimal, imperfect and impermanent.* There is a deep appreciation for life, for the small, simple, and beautiful, when we walk slowly. We can see beauty in imperfections and find an appreciation for the time, history, and life that expresses the fullness of an experience or person. *Wabi-sabi* is the beauty in the freckles and wrinkles, the black cast-iron teapot, the lone, elegant flower. It is an appreciation for the authentic, simple, and true. We feel grateful for the moment that doesn't last; there is a deep knowing that what is limited is precious..

Observations from my own life, as well as from helping others, have taught me that our culture has a high bar for perfection and that we, as a society, strive to look and be "perfect." Movies, commercials, and social media perpetuate the illusion of perfection—looking happy, successful, flawless, beautiful. This creates an unrealistic, unobtainable, and warped sense of beauty, happiness, and success. *Wabi-sabi* is a refreshingly realistic view of how we see our physical bodies, relationships, families, experiences, and work.

We can apply *wabi-sabi* in the ways we see and accept ourselves. Look at what makes you unique. See imperfection as part of what makes you beautiful. View movies, magazines, and social media with an honest lens, appreciating imperfections, valuing authenticity. Markings of age reveal a story, and we can view them as a way to honor our history. In nature, an old tree with branches missing tells of a past storm it survived. In our nature, scars and wrinkles tell tales of pain and joy; without them, we would not be our full selves.

Wabi-sabi is a way of being that is accepting, genuine, simple, and mindful. A mindful walk in nature becomes an opportunity to practice seeing beauty. The *imperfection* in beautifully battered driftwood, its history marked with cuts and imprints from years of being tumbled in water and left to dry on the shore. The beautiful *impermanence* of a fading leaf's destiny to one day let go. The *incompleteness* of the dried river channel that did not reach the ocean and now leaves prints and designs in the sand.

This philosophy applies not only to nature but to our living spaces; beauty is expressed in the minimal and simple. The blank wall with one work of art. One treasured keepsake on the desk. One elegant flower in a thin vase alone on a bare table. A beautiful contrast with filling a room with things, a desk piled with books and papers, flower arrangements everywhere.

We can train the eye to slow down and value what is beautiful in its simplicity and imperfections. I invite you to see this beauty in yourself and others and appreciate the gifts and gentle acceptance of authentic beauty that *wabi-sabi* brings into your life.

Pare down to the essence, but don't remove the poetry.
— Leonard Koren

Slow and Mindful

Take time to sip coffee or tea. Smell the aroma; feel the cup in your hands. Enjoy the simple pleasure of the mindful moment (rather than multitasking).

Simple and Minimal

Clear off a counter, desktop, or kitchen table. Take everything off except one piece of art, one plant or flower. Notice how your eye is drawn differently to this space.

Imperfection

Practice looking at yourself, your friends, your family, and identify with your hair, your body, your grades, your salary... What is authentic and uniquely beautiful in its imperfections?

Impermanence

Observe the moments, experiences, and people in your life, knowing your time here and together is limited and precious.

Practice:

Choose one, two, or all four of these practices to bring the beauty of *wabi-sabi* living into your day.

Reflection:

Journal and document when you start to observe *wabi-sabi* in the way you see beauty, think, and live.

For Your Library:

Wabi-Sabi for Artists, Designers, Poets & Philosophers by Leonard Koren

Wabi Sabi: Japanese Wisdom for a Perfectly Imperfect Life by Beth Kempton

Watch:

Hear Diana's reviews of wabi-sabi books from her personal library at www.DianaChristinson.com

DAY 32
Kintsugi

The world breaks every one and afterward many are strong at the broken places.
          —Ernest Hemingway

The act of seeing beauty in imperfections is expressed through the art of golden joinery, the Japanese art of repairing broken, fractured pottery and art with gold lacquer. This form of art is centuries old. Rather than repair ceramic pieces with a clear glue to restore a piece as closely as possible to its original form, the repair is made with gold dust in the glue to highlight the area of break or fracture.

The story of *kintsugi* dates back to the late fifteenth century. According to legend, a respected Japanese shogun, Ashikaga Yoshimasa, broke his cherished Chinese tea bowl. He sent it back to China to undergo repairs, and the bowl was returned repaired with metal staples. Displeased, he hired a local craftsman to repair the bowl with art and beauty. The craftsman joined the broken pieces together with a lacquer mixed with gold dust. The golden cracks highlighted the break and brought unique beauty to the tea bowl. It also created a new art form, *kintsugi*. By the seventeenth century, *kintsugi* had become common practice in Japan; today, it is an elegant art form that has spread and is practiced all over the world. More than just a form of repair and an art, *kintsugi* is a philosophy for living.

In contrast to the practice of discarding broken pieces of pottery, this unique repair gives the art a new life. It enhances and celebrates the unique history, using gold to honor fractures and breaks instead of hiding or disguising them. The colorful cracks and lines of *kintsugi* often make the repaired piece even more beautiful.

The origin of this art is an extension of the Japanese philosophy *wabi-sabi*, honoring beauty in the flawed or imperfect. Kintsugi was also born from the Japanese concept of *mottainai,* which expresses regret when something is wasted, as well as *mushin*, the acceptance of change. Keeping what is broken and honoring change is at the heart of the philosophy of golden repair.

Kintsugi reminds us that we are all cracked and fractured—a beautiful metaphor for our wounds, failures, and sufferings. The cracks mended with gold are a reminder that we are as much our pain as we are our joy. We honor our history and authenticity and celebrate our uniqueness by accepting the cracks and fractures of our full selves.

> Using kintsugi as a metaphor for healing ourselves and embracing our own flaws and imperfections teaches us an important lesson: Sometimes in the process of repairing things that have broken, we actually create something that is even more unique, resilient and beautiful.
>
> Those who have scars only become more powerful because of them. We don't get through life unharmed, and it's far less painful to display your scars than to continuously try to cover them. The Japanese art of Kintsugi is a tribute to us and it is SCREAMING that it does not matter if we are damaged! Once we have mended the pieces, we will be far more beautiful than ever before.
>
> —"From Broken to Beautiful: The Power of Kintsugi"
> (*Concrete Unicorn*, June 2018)

Celebrate your cracks, fractures, history—all of you. Honor your broken parts that allow the light to get in.

Reflection:

Reflect on and journal your history. Open your heart and mind to review your unique life story and where your spirit became scarred or cracked. Journal how these cracks have made you who you are today.

Practice:

Gratitude Meditation: Place your hand over your heart. For each finger, touch your heart and identify a crack that has made you who you are today and offer gratitude.

For Your Library:

Kintsugi Wellness: The Japanese Art of Nourishing Mind, Body, and Spirit by Candice Kumai

DAY 33
Plant a Garden

You must find your own garden.
       —Nelson Mandela

One of my heroes, Nelson Mandela, planted gardens during his years in prison. In the 1970s, he started a garden in the Robben Island prison. In 1982, he moved to Pollsmoor Prison and created a rooftop vegetable garden.

> *While others were playing games, Mandela was gardening.*
> *He shared produce with prisoners and guards.*
> *He quieted his mind.*
> *Surrounded by death and decay,*
> *Mandela found a place to touch beauty.*
> *Gardening was life-affirming and creative.*
> *This was not a retreat but a renewal,*
> *and helped him sustain his work in service to others.*
>
> —Jarem Sawatsky, *Dancing with Elephants*

The garden was a way for Mandela not only to survive in prison but to thrive while incarcerated. It was a way to turn his mind from hopelessness to possibility.

Therapeutic gardens have been used in hospitals for thousands of years. Many facilities—cancer centers, shelters, hospices—use gardening as part of their treatment to help people recover and heal. Nature is medicine.

Two Examples of Using Gardens to Bring Joy and Happiness into Our Lives

What a gift when my friend brings me peaches from her tree. *Ahh*, the taste, better than candy. Better than any peaches I buy from the store, they're organic, delicious, and grown with love. I realize the joy she receives from her garden: it's her therapy and a delight to share her harvest with friends.

My deck is filled with plants, lush, green, vibrant flowering bushes and trees. I feel a special joy in my small herb garden, the

> mint, basil, sage a delight to my senses. Tonight for dinner: pasta with fresh basil picked from a stem right into my bowl. Food for my soul. I am deeply nourished by these leaves I have grown.

The simple act of planting a seed and caring for your plant as it grows is a beautiful therapeutic practice for the soul.

Practice:

Create a garden. If outdoor space is limited, it can be a window box, some potted plants at your doorstep, or a rental space in a community garden. It can even be as simple as adding a small herb plant by a window or just outside your door.

Experience the joy and therapy of watching the miracle of a flower or vegetable growing. Enjoy the harvesting and the sharing. In Mandela's powerful words, **"Plant your own garden."**

Reflection:

Reflect and journal about times you have grown a fruit, vegetable, or flowering plant. It might be a memory from your childhood or perhaps a more recent experience. Was it exciting and joyful to water a plant and watch it grow? Was it therapeutic to weed and care for the plant?

For Your Library:

I recommend both of these inspirational books on the life of Nelson Mandela:

Long Walk to Freedom: The Autobiography of Nelson Mandela by Nelson Mandela

Mandela's Way: Fifteen Lessons on Life, Love, and Courage by Richard Stengel

DAY 34
"If Not Now, WHEN?"

The following short but powerful question from the Jewish Talmud is an inquiry into how we are living. It's an opportunity for self-assessment, a call to action:

If not now, when?

How are you spending today? Living in the present, dedicating slivers of time for renewing your spirit? Most people are *too busy*—doing, fixing, planning, thinking, running to their next task. How often do you say, *I just don't have enough time*? But if we petitioned the universe for one more hour a day, would we fill it the same *and still ask for more*?

As a yoga and meditation teacher, I would like to tell you I am an expert in managing my time and allowing for my simple pleasures, dreams, and passions. What I have found over the past five decades of my life is that doing so is a *practice*. If we don't begin to practice unplugging, turning off, and *choosing* to gift *ourselves* sacred time now, if we don't take the leap of faith and pursue the dream, then it becomes WHEN? And again, tomorrow and the next day.

I think this question provokes a deep inner sense of how we are living. Are we happy with our daily choices, taking time to go for a walk, turning off work before burnout, spending time with family? Or perhaps the question stirs a passion inside, bigger choices that you are afraid to pursue: writing your book, creating a new business, leaving a relationship or job.

In *The Book of Awakening*, Mark Nepo refers to our "yes, buts." Yes, but... I don't have time. I am not ready. I am not good enough yet. Familiar? What are your "yes, buts"?

To observe how we spend time is to observe what we value. Hearing a "yes, *but*" could change to an "If not now, *when*?" Remember, this is your one wild, precious life.

Reflection:

What are your "yes, buts"? Reflect and journal about what stops you from choosing how you spend the moments of your day.

What is something you have been dreaming or feel passionate about doing? As you reflect on your passions, pay attention to how it makes you feel to give this dream attention. Open the door to possibility by considering how you might begin a new dream.

Practice:

Today, when you hear yourself saying or thinking a "yes, *but*," switch your mindset to: If not now, *when*?

List two to three small things you *wish* you had more time for.

Schedule and dedicate fifteen minutes a day for one item on your list.

For Your Library:

Mark Nepo, one of my favorite authors, wrote a daily devotional book, *The Book of Awakening*, twenty-one years ago. A writer, poet, and cancer survivor, Nepo tells the reader, "It is my profound hope that something in these pages... will help you live, love, and find your way to joy."

 ## DAY 35
Lose Your Shoes

Forget not that the earth delights to feel your bare feet and the winds long to play with your hair. —Khalil Gibran

We spend too much time in our boxes, and it's making us sick. We move through our days from a house box to a box with wheels to an office box while wearing foot boxes we call shoes. We were designed to interact with our magnetic planet, to touch the earth. Our modern lives have pulled us away from the most important source of our health—the earth.

When was the last time you walked barefoot in the grass or the sand? Earthing, also referred to as grounding, is simply walking or gardening or lying on the ground with skin touching and connecting to the earth. This is how we transfer the earth's electrons from the ground into the body. Take off your shoes, walk, and notice how you feel that day. Over the years, my students have shared how their earthing practice has positively impacted their sleep, inflammation, energy, and mood.

Touching the earth with our physical bodies is not only therapeutic, it is essential. Everyone carries electric energy within their body, and we must balance the overabundance of positive electrons we get from our Wi-Fi and electronics. By physically connecting to the earth, we bring our bodies back into balance with the negative charge of the earth.

Benefits of Earthing:
- Reduces chronic pain
- Reduces inflammation
- Reduces stress
- Improves sleep
- Accelerates healing process
- Increases energy
- Elevates moods
- Improves blood flow
- Increases oxygen and nutrients to cells and tissue

From the book *Earthing*: "Reconnecting yourself to the Earth may not produce the same effect as jumpstarting a dead battery, but it does work surprisingly fast to re-energize fatigued bodies and reduce pain. Earthing usually generates a healing response that people feel after twenty to thirty minutes. Pain reduction can occur much faster."

Lose Your Shoes!

Practice:
Fifteen-minute daily practice: walk or sit in grass, sand, earth.

Feel free to extend your fifteen minutes or do multiple practices.

Reflection:
Reflect on the last time you walked barefoot or sat in the grass, sand, dirt. How did it make you feel? How did it affect your mood or your sleep? Write about your experience.

For Your Library:
This book will improve your health.

Earthing: The Most Important Health Discovery Ever! by Clinton Ober; Stephen T. Sinatra, MD; and Martin Zucker

Watch:
"*Down to Earth*," a 15-minute short from *The Earthing Movie* on www.DianaChristinson.com

Bonus:
Purchase an earthing pad or sheets to earth inside your house or office.

DAY 36

The Invisible Gift

And now here is my secret, a very simple secret: It is only with the heart that one can see rightly; what is essential is invisible to the eye. —Antoine de Saint-Exupéry

The Little Prince is a novella by French writer and aviator Antoine de Saint-Exupéry. It has been translated into one hundred languages and has touched the hearts of people of every age and culture with its story of love and loss, of loneliness and friendship. In the story, the fox and the little prince become friends. When the day arrives for the friends to say goodbye, the fox gives the little prince a gift. He tells him a special secret: *What is essential is invisible to the eye.*

This is a universal secret—it is the gift of love. It is what makes life worth living, but it must be felt from the heart. Our time together is limited—it is a priceless gift. How long do we have to share this gift? Not one of us knows the answer. We may have a long life with our loved ones, or it could be a brief time. What do we value most? Is it to love and be loved in return?

It is often at times of goodbyes that we know the true value of love. The little prince is leaving the fox, and it is at their goodbye that the fox shares the importance of their friendship and love. The greatest gifts are the gifts of the heart, and when blessed by love, that love remains after the goodbye.

There are many reasons we say goodbye—a friend moves away, we break up with our partner, a loved one dies. It is sometimes difficult to talk about goodbyes, losses, and death, but I believe talking about and contemplating loss and death are essential to how we show up and live. Being present for a loved one's last breath is a gift. We know our time together is limited, and this helps us bring more attention to the *way* we live and the *way* we love.

I know the blessing; I love my father, and our goodbye was filled with little moments of connection and deep love. I will always cherish the last weeks and days we had together, holding hands, sometimes in silence; the whisper of *I love you*. I gave him a small stone heart to hold in his hand at times I could not be there. If he lost the heart in bed, Mom would find it and return it to his hand. When I would return, I would sit by his side, hand in hand, with the heart tucked in our joined hands. After his passing, I keep the stone heart near, often carrying it in a pocket to remind me that he is always near and that our love continues and will always be with me.

When we lose someone we love, will we wish we had said "I love you" one more time? Will we wish for one more day, hour, minute together, one more sip of love?

Today, if you are blessed with the love of a partner, friend, parent, child, LOVE THEM FULLY WITH ALL YOUR HEART AND WORDS.

Reflection:

Reflect and journal about who you love. If you knew you were going to say a last goodbye, what invisible gift would you give them? How would you treat them? What would you say?

Practice:

Gratitude Meditation: Hold your hands over your heart and focus on the people you love. Fill your mind and heart with gratitude for the gift of love. Say thank you.

Bonus: Tell them you love them, and tell them as often as possible.

For Your Library:

The Little Prince by Antoine de Saint-Exupéry

This is one of my top five favorite books of all time. It is as much for adults as it is for children.

DAY 37
How We Spend Today

How we spend our days is, of course, how we spend our lives. —Annie Dillard

I remember a wooden plaque that hung on our bathroom wall from the time I could read, a print of a little girl skipping with a doll in her hand and a big smile on her face. It said, "May you live all the days of your life." That piece of art went with us from Michigan to Indiana. I remember seeing it on the wall when I was in high school. It was still hanging there when I returned home from university, and it even managed to show up when my parents moved to California thirty years later. I can still see it clearly in my mind. When I was a little girl, it was a joyful image; now that I am a woman, seasoned from years of living and loving, it has a timeless message. Make the most of each precious day. Live joyfully, live fully, this day and every day.

This life is our journey. Remember that we are the stars of our stories. We are the heroes and heroines of the adventures. It is our choice whether to show up each day and live fully. We make opportunities to follow our dreams, take risks, and stand strong in the inevitable challenges of life.

A quote on my desk reads, "What would you do if you knew you could not fail?" It's a reminder to take risks, fall down, get back up, learn and grow. A reminder to live fully—there are lessons in failure.

Living fully means recognizing small treasures and gifts each day brings. Did I skip, like the child in the print, or did I drag myself through the day? Living the moments could be planning small details of a big dream, a spontaneous walk to get ice cream, an afternoon out in nature, enjoying a good book.

That simple plaque is a theme and inspiration for how we spend our days. To Annie Dillard's quote I add, **How we spend our moments is how we spend our days**. Be aware and choose how you want to spend your moments. Will you choose a walk outside instead of starting your day with the news? Coffee with a friend instead of scrolling social media? Watching the night sky instead of the TV? Remember the Chinese saying *yi ke qian jin*, "time is precious."

Reflection:

How do you want to spend your day today? What is stopping you from doing it?

    List three ways to skip and move joyfully through the day.

    List three ways you drag yourself through the day.

Practice:

Use your list and make choices to increase your skipping and joyfulness today.

DAY 38
What If?

"Why, sometimes I've believed as many as six impossible things before breakfast."
—Lewis Carroll, *Alice in Wonderland*

What was your first thought when you woke up today? What were you thinking while brushing your teeth? Were you excited about the day ahead? Like Alice, were you dreaming up ideas, passionate about the possibilities of the day?

A few years back, I started to write a book I titled *What If?* These two words followed by a question mark open a door to a world of passions, possibilities, adventures, creations—or they can open a door to fear, worry, skepticism, and CREATION of the very things we fear. After years of studying and practicing psychology, I have observed that the way people finish this question is fundamental to the lives they create and live.

We are often unconscious and on autopilot, living our *What Ifs*. Becoming skillful in choosing the possibilities of the day requires becoming an observer. Notice: pay attention to your inner voice, your habitual patterns of thinking, doing, and being. Once we can *Catch a Thought*, we can change it.

My book idea, *What If*, has become a living investigation. I see these two words as an opportunity to wake up my personal life muse and be inspired to dream. Are you creating a *What If* of fear or a *What If* that makes you smile? A dream that leads to a new idea?

Lord, grant that I may always desire more than I can accomplish.
—Michelangelo

Michelangelo and Lewis Carroll inspire us to show up excited about life. There is an art to living our passions and creating adventure and possibility in our life stories. Dream *more* than you can accomplish, and start your day with six impossible things.

Create the day you want to live.

Reflection:

Reflect on your life story and make a list of impossible things you imagined and brought into being. Now create a new list. What will you imagine for today and tomorrow?

Practice:

Flip It!

As you make coffee, brush your teeth, drive to work—observe your thinking. If you find yourself creating a day filled with worry and problems, *Flip It*.

Catch the thought, pull it back in your head, and turn it upside down.

Worry can be reimagined into a hope-filled *What If,* a shift to see possibilities instead of problems.

Try it, and then try it again.

DAY 39

Awaken from Your Sensory Slumber

I think it pisses God off if you walk by the color purple in a field somewhere and don't notice it.
　　—Alice Walker, *The Color Purple*

Have you ever driven home and weren't sure how you got there? Walked a path without noticing a single tree? There are moments and days we sleepwalk through beauty, awe, magic, and love. Are we so weary that we operate on autopilot, blind to the miracles around us? Is it possible to be bored of the magnificence of nature or our lives?

In the movie *The Color Purple*, two friends are walking through a field and one of them is noticing the flowers, their majestic color. This scene and Alice Walker's words remind me to pay attention, to be grateful.

At times I have been awoken from my sensory slumber by a smell, a sound, or a vibrant color. On my way home from work one spring day, I was delighted by the library lawn, a vibrant green sprinkled with bright-yellow dandelions. It was nature's green blanket patterned with hundreds of happy yellow polka dots. I smiled and declared out loud, *"Beautiful!"* While public declarations are perhaps an unusual display of simple joy at the sight of yellow flowers, speaking my gratitude aloud woke me up to feeling awe, appreciation, and joy.

Today, I declare **thank you** for a golden-orange sunset, purple lavender, unique dragonflies, the sound of a hummingbird's wings, the smell of a pine tree, well-dressed ladybugs, soaring red-tailed hawks, the magical sound of wind chimes.

Reflection:

What are you noticing and grateful for today? Nature's abundant gifts surround you.

How can you wake up to the beauty around you and let it inspire you?

Practice:
Express your gratitude for the gifts in nature. Write it, say it, share it.

Alice Walker—a former editor of Ms. magazine and the daughter of sharecroppers—published The Color Purple in 1982. It was the first work by a Black woman to win both the Pulitzer and National Book awards.

 **DAY 40**

The We of Me

...and it was as though when first she saw them something she had known inside of her: They are the we of me.
    —Carson McCullers,
        The Member of the Wedding

We Are the People We Love.

In high school, I had saved enough money to buy a sailboat. Mind you, I had no idea how to sail, but my best friend and I decided to learn together. Ali and I were like two peas in a pod of joy, having fun as we navigated our way through trial and error. Our many adventures included early fishing excursions to the Lake Michigan pier. We often forgot bait or sinkers; the *real* fishermen laughed and tried to help us. We never caught any fish, but it didn't matter, because we had donuts, coffee, and each other! Ali and I could talk about anything and everything. We were coconspirators, ready to save the world. She gave me the book *The Tao of Pooh*, knowing how much I loved the butterfly-chasing bear. I still have and cherish this book; it is one of the few books that have traveled with me and will be in my library for life.

I was in college when I met Hannah on the dorm rooftop—*the* sunning spot for freshmen to work on their '80s tans. I noticed the cardboard bridge she had created to cover her nose. I was intrigued and had to ask, "What is on your nose?" Her creative sunscreen led to this serendipitous encounter that brought us together. We laughed and have been friends ever since. Hannah is a soul friend. She, too, gifted me with a cherished book, *A Pilgrim at Tinker Creek*, by Annie Dillard, which traveled with me to many homes over the years. It is well loved and worn, waterlogged from multiple readings in multiple bathtubs. Hannah is the friend who encouraged me to learn and recite poetry, express my passions, debate, be nutty and silly. We listened to R.E.M. and U2, and we, *too*, conspired to save the world.

Someone once said, "If you want to know who you are, look around you—who do you surround yourself with, who are your friends? They are a mirror, they are a reflection of you."

Ali and Hannah are reflections of the best of me—my beloved friends from my teens and twenties, soul friends for life. They are part of the fiber of my being, the way I choose a book, laugh, experience what deep friendship feels like. We are the people we love. These two women are part of my history and my present. I could not possibly be completely me today if I had not met and loved them.

My friends still want to save the world, still save *me* at times, and share literature, adventure, laughter, and inspiration. My mom, dad, brother, and dearest friends are all part of the colorful textures of my life's tapestry. They are all a part of the unique fiber of me.

**Look around you.
Celebrate the people who are part of your fiber, your WE!**

Reflection:

Reflect and journal about your earliest memories of your *We*. Who are the people—family, friends, teachers—who have influenced who you are today? Write a list of your friends from elementary school, high school, college, or your first job. How are they part of your *Me*? Make a list of the friends and family who surround you today—they are your mirror.

Practice:

Gratitude Meditation: Place a hand over your heart and picture five people who are a part of the fiber of you. For each finger, focus on one person and how they have influenced your life. Send gratitude and blessings. Repeat.

Have ten people in mind? Place both hands over your heart!

Bonus: Tell them! Thank them with a note, simple message, phone call, or visit.

Watch:

Join Diana as she leads you through a loving kindness Metta Meditation on www.DianaChristinson.com

DAY 41

A Message from a Wasp

I like insects for their stupidity. A paper wasp is fumbling at a stained glass window on my right. I saw the same sight in the same spot last Sunday. Psst! Idiot! Sweetheart! Go around by the door! I hope we seem as endearingly stupid to God—bumbling down into lamps, running half-wit across the floor, banging for days at the hinge of an opened door. —Annie Dillard

Today, I was the wasp. Writing, rewriting, deleting, starting over—nothing worked. I was banging and fumbling at the stained glass window, feeling stuck and irritated. When I shared my frustration with my wise mom, she advised, "Stop writing and go for a walk on the beach." I resisted initially, continuing to attempt to force my creativity, continuing to hit my head. Once I caught myself, I gave in to good advice and turned my computer off, put my sneakers on, and headed for the beach.

On the way down the hill, I started thinking of what to do with my writing, what possible new ideas I could explore. I noticed I was back in my head, as if still at my computer, and in *noticing*, I found the space in between, the pause. I listened and imagined my mom's voice urging me, "Stop! Unplug!"

I walked through the neighborhood, noticing the flowers in bloom, the sound of the birds chirping. A few deep breaths, and I began to feel more light, open, and happy.

Walking down the stairs, I saw the bright, crystal-blue water and smelled the ocean. I smiled and took a few deep breaths. As I listened to the powerful sound of the waves crashing, the warm sand

and cool water delighted my bare feet. I thought *Lucky Me* as I enjoyed a slow walk down the shore.

On the way home, I picked wildflowers and continued my thoughts of gratitude. Once home, I put my flowers in my favorite vase, placing them in the kitchen window near where I had been writing. I turned on some music and poured a cup of coffee. No longer irritated, I felt fresh and ready for some creative inspiration. My beach walk had been an unplug and reset, medicine for my body and fatigued mind.

Today, I practiced:
- Pausing to create space in between
- Locating myself
- Forest bathing
- *Wabi-sabi*
- Bringing the outdoors in
- Deep breathing
- Energy banking

It works! Today I am the wasp who used a few of my own practices and found my way out the open door. Incorporating even just *one* of these practices when in a frustrating situation can show us the door that's been open all along.

In this universal metaphor, we can all relate to the wasp, hitting our head against a problem with fixed thinking. Feeling stuck in a loop can prevent us from seeing new possibilities and open doors. *Psst!* Remind yourself of the practices that can open doors to new solutions and opportunities.

Practice:

Observe when you are stuck. Catch your fixed thinking, the negative loop, and apply one or two of these practices:

- Pausing to create space in between
- Locating myself
- Forest bathing

- *Wabi-sabi*
- Bringing the outdoors in
- Deep breathing
- Energy banking

Reflection:

Reflect on times you have felt like the wasp banging your head against an open door.

Reflect and journal about the moments when you used one of your practices to change a negative loop.

DAY 42
Influencers

We Are the Ones We've Been Waiting For.
             —Hopi Elders' Prophecy

I was recently introduced to the term *influencer*, describing people who have a strong online presence and following on social media. The influencer can inspire subscribers' views as well as purchases. I was immediately intrigued. My mind went to all the hundreds and thousands of people who have influenced my life. My courage and sense of adventure came from my father, my spirituality and faith from my mom. I have my brother's taste in music and art, my high school teacher's love for literature, my college coworker's fascination with self-study and personal growth. Pause for a moment and reflect on how many people have touched your life and in some way influenced the person you are today. Strangers, family, people you knew for a brief or long time in your life—even the people whose actions or way of being influenced how you did *not* want to be.

> *Research into social networks has shown that behavior is literally contagious, good or bad. Our attitudes and behaviors infect the people we work with directly, but also spread to the people they interact with. This is called the ripple effect.*
>
> —Shawn Achor, *The Happiness Advantage*

The word *influencer* also inspires me to reflect on how I influence others, often unintentionally, just by my actions and the way I show up. We don't need a large online following—we are all influencers. Our actions can affect our friends, children, coworkers... The list is infinite. Research has proven that the way you dress, talk, or treat someone can influence a friend or stranger, and your reach is farther than you think.

In the book *Connected: The Surprising Power of Our Social Networks and How They Shape Our Lives*, by James H. Fowler and Nicholas Christakis, the research shows that our actions are constantly bouncing off each other. We all agree that our actions can directly impact the health and happiness of our friends and family, but Fowler and Christakis explain how an individual's impact extends far beyond our close social circle. Most of us influence people within three degrees of ourselves, which they estimated to be nearly one thousand people.

> *In a kind of social chain reaction, we can be deeply affected by events we do not witness that happen to people we do not know. It is as if we can feel the pulse of the social world around us and respond to its persistent rhythms. As part of a social network, we transcend ourselves, for good or ill, and become a part of something much larger. We are connected... Ties do not extend outward in straight lines like spokes on a wheel. Instead, these paths double down on themselves and spiral around like a tangled pile of spaghetti, weaving in and out of other paths that rarely ever leave the plate.*
>
> —James H. Fowler and Nicholas Christakis, *Connected*

These complex connections can be seen in everyday situations we can all relate to. Consider the following scenario:

You kiss your loved one and say, "Have a great day! I love you." Afterward, as they interact with coworkers and clients, they are in a great mood from the feeling of being loved: upbeat, funny, giving compliments. A frustrated client is on the phone to resolve an issue, and rather than getting irritated and frustrated, your loved one is calm and understanding as they consider possible solutions. The client becomes appreciative and is kinder in their next interaction.

Now take the same moment, but rather than kiss your spouse and give words of love, you snap at your partner, become irritated, and say something hurtful. They go to work angry and irritated, spreading discontent not only in the office but on the phone with clients as well. Now the client's frustration with your partner grows and extends into their next interaction. This simple example of the tangled-spaghetti effect illustrates how one moment can affect so many other people in their moments.

Mahatma Gandhi touched and inspired millions and continues to influence people to this day. He said "My life is my message" and encouraged us to "be the change you want to see in the world." You are an influencer. Your life today can potentially influence thousands of people. Be the change you want to see in the world. Let your life be a message of love and hope. Let your laughter, kindness, and optimism be contagious. Find opportunities throughout your days to spread love and gratitude.

Reflection:

Think of your actions as a way of being. How are they influencing others? List the ways you would like your actions, words, and life to affect others.

Who did you affect yesterday? Reflect on all the people in your life who you potentially touched yesterday. Go further, and reflect on who they might have affected. See the extension of your connections of influence.

Practice:

Think of your circle of friends, family, coworkers, or neighbors. Choose two or three actions you can employ today to start a spaghetti effect that will positively influence one thousand people.

Watch:

Ted Talk: *The Hidden Influence of Social Networks* with Nicholas Christakis on www.DianaChristinson.com

DAY 43
Happiness Is an Inside Job

Everything can be taken from a man but one thing: the last of the human freedoms—to choose one's attitude in any given set of circumstances, to choose one's own way.
—Viktor Frankl

At the core of my being, I believe happiness is an inside job. Life circumstances can *affect* but do not *determine* happiness. When we look at Frankl, we can see that when his life circumstances were horrific, he chose to be strong, hopeful, and encouraging toward others. His life story teaches us that life circumstances do not define us; we always have the power to choose our own way.

Every day, we have opportunities to choose an optimistic thought over a negative one, a possibility over a worry. The way we cope with life situations and stress trains our brain. Daily worry makes us expert worriers. Our choice to *not* worry then becomes our power to redirect our thoughts to hope and opportunity, to *Flip It* and redirect the mind to happiness. The external life situations we face strongly influence the reality we create in the mind. When we choose the thought we want to have, we create our happiness *from the inside*. British essayist Erich Heller wrote, "**Be careful how you interpret the world: it is like that.**" The quality of your thoughts becomes the quality of your life.

According to Shawn Achor, "Our external circumstances predict only about 10% of our total happiness." This is incredibly good news! This means the other 90 percent of our happiness is cultivated within. This is evidence that the good and the bad, our joys and our challenges, do not determine our happiness—we do. Ninety percent of your joy and contentment *is an inside job*. You create your happiness.

When you can create a *space in between*, a distinction between life happening and your response, you can reenvision a bigger perspective. Retrain your mind to move from patterns of knee-jerk reactivity and strong emotions to thoughtful responses from a place of calm understanding.

A situation might break you down, or the same one could build you up. **YOU choose**.

Reflection:

Calculate your waking hours, which likely take up between sixteen and eighteen hours of each day. How many hours out of the day would you like to be happy? Define your happiness. What does it look and feel like to you? Create a list of happy feelings and situations.

Practice:

Take one item from your happiness list and add it to your day. Begin with small changes.

Use the skills you've **been practicing:**

Meditate and practice **gratitude**.

Connect with nature.

Catch a Thought, then **Flip It**.

DAY 44

Love and Happiness

When all your desires are distilled
You will cast just two votes:
To love more, and be happy.
                    —Hafiz

This was meant to be one of the quotes shared at my wedding to Richard. Instead, I read these words from Hafiz at Richard's celebration of life. Our time together was just getting started, our path unfolding, our love growing. Richard was healthy, vibrant, and young; his passing was unexpected. He was diagnosed with brain cancer and died forty-eight days later. At his service, I shared the Hafiz quote. It's a reminder: *when all our life's desires are distilled*, as we take our last breath, we will sense deeply what was most important. Life and love are a privilege; to love and be loved is the greatest of gifts.

After Richard's passing, I didn't want to take an hour or day for granted, nor did I want to waste my precious energy on petty, small things. I felt a change in what I viewed as priorities, in what I valued most. I made a commitment that I renew every New Year's Day—my vow to be the best lover of life and people for the rest of my days. I felt called to urge everyone, as if I had discovered the secret meaning of life, *make the most of each day, and LOVE every chance you get! Love is the biggest and most precious gift.*

We are shaped and fashioned by what we love.
       —Johann Wolfgang von Goethe

My loss also gave me a renewed appreciation for the things I may take for granted that bring daily happiness to my life. Often, I realize it's the simplest things that I value most. To remind myself of what is most valuable, I copied a dollar bill, and on the back, I wrote a list of things I love that bring me happiness and joy. I tucked it into a special place—my wallet. I see it as I pull out a credit card or cash, a reminder of what makes my life rich.

On the back, I wrote:

The smell of coffee, holding hands, the sound of rain, the smell of rain, a kiss, the moon setting over the ocean, the nightingale's song at night, the feeling of snuggling into bed, saying the words *I love you*, **hearing the words** *I love you*...

Our *true wealth* is seen in the people we love as well as the rich experiences and everyday moments that bring us happiness.

Reflection:

What would you write on the back of a dollar to remind you of your true wealth, the most important gifts? What would fill your list? How will you define true wealth?

Practice:

On the back of a copied dollar bill, write the things you love. Write a list of the people, things, and experiences that bring you joy. Keep this bill in your wallet as a reminder of your true wealth.

DAY 45
You Are the Hero

Life has no meaning. Each of us has meaning and we bring it to life. It is a waste to be asking the question when you are the answer. People say that what we're all seeking is a meaning for life. I don't think that's what we're really seeking. I think that what we're seeking is an experience of being alive, so that our life experiences on the purely physical plane will have resonances with our own innermost being and reality, so that we actually feel the rapture of being alive.

—Joseph Campbell

You are the hero, the heroine of your life story. You are also the writer and the director. We know this, but we forget. It is often in the midst of a life storm that we forget this is our adventure. We are the star, and yet we cast ourselves as the victim of life's circumstances, life's challenges.

Joseph Campbell mapped out mythology from many cultures and time periods. Studying these legends is fascinating, and the nuggets of universal truth within them inspire me and my teachings. As a yoga teacher, I studied Hindu mythology, and the story of the monkey king, Hanuman, is one of my personal favorites. Hanuman was born with many superpowers, but as a young monkey, he was a mischievous one, constantly getting in trouble. After he attempted to fly up and swallow the sun, the lords decided young Hanuman should be cursed to forget his powers. His distraught father begged the lords to reconsider, but they vowed that he would not remember his superstrength, his ability to fly and transform and be the hero, until reminded by another. By performing feats of strength, devotion, and courage, Hanuman was reminded and rediscovered his gifts. In his many adventures, Hanuman found the strength and power to save the day.

I like to share Hanuman's tale because it is a curse, a glitch, inherent in all of us. We don't remember our strength and abilities, our heroism within. It is a universal story: we often forget what we have within ourselves at life's most challenging moments. I think of the words by Marianne Williamson that remind us to ask ourselves: "Who am I to be brilliant, gorgeous, talented, fabulous? Actually, who are you not to be?... Your playing small doesn't serve the world."

In my years of teaching the Hero's Journey, I have often reminded students of their gifts. Our life is our journey. If you don't like the story you are living, talk to the writer—you. I remind myself that every story has challenges, traumas, loss, and love. We love, we break our hearts, but what would life be without love? A life would not be fully lived without a broken heart or two. *Kintsugi* reminds us to go out in the world and get cracked: let your heart be broken, and repair it with gold.

Hanuman's story reminds us that, no matter what life brings, we have the strength and power to show up as the hero. The trick to living your life as the star of your story is in remembering your gifts. *You have the skills and the tenacity.*

On your life's journey, pack for your adventure:

- Compass: Locate yourself and navigate from your true north.
- Gold coin: *Yi ke qian jin*; remember, moments are golden.
- Glasses: *How* you see determines *what* you see.
- Heart: Love is the greatest gift.
- Detour sign: Flip It; change your view.
- Rain boots: Dance in the rain and express joy.
- Superhero figure: Remember, you are the hero or heroine of your story.

These items are symbols representing continued inspirations on your journey. I surround myself with symbolic touchstones to remind me of my intentions: a compass at my school, a heart in my pocket, and a gold coin in my wallet all inspire me at different times to remember what's important in the daily moments of my life—my life's path. I invite you to join me and fill your pockets and homes and surround yourself with touchstones to inspire you on your continued Golden Journey of Life.

Reflection:

What are your superpowers, your strength, skills, personal assets? How do you use them in being the hero or heroine of your life adventure? How can you remind yourself of your skills and gifts in the moments of your day?

Practice:

Take one or two of these items and physically place them in your home or office to serve as reminders as you continue your journey forward.

- Compass
- Gold coin
- Glasses
- Heart
- Detour sign
- Rain boots
- A superhero

The Gift

There have always and will always be the challenges that we humans face. As animals we walk the earth. As bearers of a divine essence, we are among the stars. As human beings, we are caught in the middle, seeking to reconcile the paradox of how to make our way on earth while striving for something more permanent and more profound. So many seek this greater Truth in the heavens, but it lies much closer than the clouds. It is within us and can be found by anyone on the Inward Journey.

—B. K. S. Iyengar

Congratulations on the completion of your forty-five-day pilgrimage. I honor your commitment to self-study and personal exploration. May this six-week journey continue to remind you that *you* are the hero or heroine, star and writer, of your life story. I also hope that this special time of reflection and inspiration will continue to remind you that your life is your journey, your great adventure, and that you direct your path.

I invite you to continue starting your day with your Golden Practice and devoting sacred time to yourself. Revisit the journey when you are ready for more growth and change. Share the journey with a friend, partner, or family member, and commit to the journey together. You can use *Your Golden Journey* for daily or weekly inspiration. Let it remind you of your golden potential on your path of life.

Use the inspirations and practices: Catch a Thought, create space in between, unplug and reset. Continue to practice sacred time, gratitude, and Lucky Me moments. Remember the ten-thousand-hour theory—it's in the continued practice that you will become better at living your life from the inside out and moving deeper into your gold.

My intention was to give you simple teachings that would transform how you show up for life. My hope was that you would make time for yourself and cultivate a self-love and deep knowing that would allow you to live your life from the inside out.

I leave you with this gift: the practice.

It is now *your* practice. It belongs to you. Each day of your life is precious. Use your Golden Practice to travel inward, locate yourself, and navigate your way through your one wild, precious life.

You may fall off at times and lose your practice. I hope you hear my loving words: "It's okay; just wake up tomorrow and give yourself a little time." Let the practice grow. Be kind to yourself.

 DAY 46

Let the Journey Continue

Unfold your own myth.
—Rumi

Thank you for going on this pilgrimage with me. It has been an honor to be your guide and teacher and to walk this path with you. Blessings on your continued journey.

One Thousand Gratitudes
Itadakimasu いただきます

May the gratitude in my heart kiss all the universe. —Hafiz

Itadakimasu is a Japanese phrase, used before eating a meal, that translates to "I humbly receive" but can also be interpreted as "bless all the hands of those who cultivated and prepared the food." This phrase has ties to the Buddhist principle of respecting all living things and reminds us to be mindful of all of the people and work that helped bring food to the table.

I remember asking my friend in Japan the meaning of the word, and she explained that it is saying thank you to the cook, the farmers, the truck driver, the dishwashers, the land, and the water for giving us this food. The depth of meaning behind *itadakimasu* influenced how I offer gratitude for my food and taught me a way of seeing a deeper, wider view of the people and things I am truly blessed by.

I think of the teachings on influencers. How many people have influenced my life and supported me in the writing and publishing of *Your Golden Journey*? Remembering all the people who have touched my life and impacted the writing of this book, I could easily thank a thousand people for their love, support, and contribution to my journey.

I humbly thank my students and private clients, who inspire all of my teachings, including the forty-five-day Golden Journey. I am eternally grateful for each one of you, and none of these teachings would exist without you.

Thank you to my dear friends, the *we*s of *me*, who have walked this path with me for many years. You are in my fiber and in the pages of this book, and you know me at my core. Your love, support, and faith are a cherished gift.

My happy gratitude goes to my two furry soul companions, Sasha and Tehya, who are always at my side. Writing was more joyful and included more laughter and love with you near me.

Let the beauty of what you love be what you do.

——Rumi

I absolutely love what I do, and this book is forty-five days of practices I love and continue to do. It is a dream realized if I can make you smile and make your day a little better with simple joy and reminders of your golden self. I thank the people who have allowed me to share these inspirations, especially my Launch Team readers and my dream team of experts—Jennifer Geist, Elyse Lyon, and Heather Hellmann.

A special thank-you to the people who helped me give life to *Your Golden Journey*:

My father is the inspiration to follow my heart and my dreams. His optimism and gratitude live on through me and these pages, and it is our love that brought this book into the world.

My mother is the beautiful spirit. Her devotion to her faith has been my lifelong inspiration. She gifted me a view of the soul, the inside of myself, and a path to find my own spirituality. Her inward beauty continues to be a light and inspiration on my path.

Jenny Soto-Banks is the magician who helped to organize and complete the book. Her patience, tenacity, dedication, and artful writing and editing skills were a gift, and she was instrumental in giving the teachings a new language and translating my voice into writing.

Lorna Moy-Masaki is the artist who brought the book to life with her beautiful eye for design. The cover, the art within the book, and the format she created are an extraordinary expression of the content of the journey. She took my vision and created a work of art beyond anything I could've imagined.

Beverly is the digital manager extraordinaire who has brought many of my passion projects to life. She artfully projects the essence of the content in a way that perfectly represents what is at the heart of my inspirations and teachings.

Markus Gerszi is the visionary coach who gave this project a plan of action. He challenged me to break out of boxes, shift old patterns of limitation, and dream and live bigger. His guidance has brought me to new, exciting places on my heroine's journey.

Richard, I am eternally grateful your love continues to support my dreams and open doors. Our time on this planet was short, but your presence is forever, which is how long I will love you.

> *The true lover is the one who on your final day opens a thousand doors.*
>
> —Rumi

Gratefully, Diana

Reference List

Books

Achor, Shawn. *The Happiness Advantage: How a Positive Brain Fuels Success in Work and Life*. New York: Currency, 2010.

Allen, James. *As a Man Thinketh*. Eastford, CT: Martino Fine Books, 2018. First published 1913 by Thomas Y. Crowell (New York).

Baum, L. Frank. *The Wonderful Wizard of Oz*. Orinda, CA: SeaWolf Press, 2019. First published 1900 by George M. Hill (Chicago).

Bstan-'dzin-rgya-mtsho [Dalai Lama XIV] and Desmond Tutu with Douglas Abrams. *The Book of Joy: Lasting Happiness in a Changing World*. New York: Avery, 2016.

Campbell, Joseph. *The Hero's Journey: Joseph Campbell on His Life and Work*. Edited and with an introduction by Phil Cousineau. Collected Works of Joseph Campell. Novato, CA: New World Library, 2003.

Campbell, Joseph with Bill Moyers. *The Power of Myth*. Edited by Betty Sue Flowers. New York: Anchor, 1991.

Carroll, Lewis. *Alice in Wonderland*. Edited by Donald J. Gray. Norton Critical Editions. 3rd ed. New York: W. W. Norton, 2013.

Christakis, Nicholas and James H. Fowler. *Connected: The Surprising Power of Our Social Networks and How They Shape Our Lives*. New York: Little, Brown, 2009.

Dillard, Annie. *Pilgrim at Tinker Creek*. New York: Harper Perennial Modern Classics, 2013.

———. *Teaching a Stone to Talk: Expeditions and Encounters*. New York: Harper Perennial, 2013.

Frankl, Viktor. *Man's Search for Meaning*. Part one translated by Ilse Lasch. Boston: Beacon Press, 2006.

Gladwell, Malcolm. *Outliers: The Story of Success*. New York: Little, Brown, 2008.

Hoff, Benjamin. *The Tao of Pooh*. New York: Dutton, 1982.

Israel, Dorien. *Unbound: The Cycle of Ascendancy; How Your Life Evolves around It*. Victoria, BC: Trafford, 2006.

———. *The Way Home: Tao Passages*. Reston, VA: Willow Way, 1997.

Iyengar, B. K. S. with John J. Evans and Douglas Carlton Abrams. *Light on Life: The Yoga Journey to Wholeness, Inner Peace, and Ultimate Freedom*. Emmaus, PA: Rodale, 2006.

Kempton, Beth. *Wabi Sabi: Japanese Wisdom for a Perfectly Imperfect Life*. New York: Harper Design, 2019.

Kingston, Karen. *Clear Your Clutter with Feng Shui: Free Yourself from Physical, Mental, Emotional, and Spiritual Clutter Forever*. Rev. ed. New York: Harmony, 2013.

Kondo, Marie. *The Life-Changing Magic of Tidying Up: The Japanese Art of Decluttering and Organizing*. Berkeley, CA: Ten Speed, 2014.

Koren, Leonard. *Wabi-Sabi for Artists, Designers, Poets & Philosophers*. Point Reyes, CA: Imperfect Publishing, 2008.

Kornfield, Jack. *The Wise Heart: A Guide to the Universal Teachings of Buddhist Psychology*. New York: Bantam, 2008.

Kumai, Candice. *Kintsugi Wellness: The Japanese Art of Nourishing Mind, Body, and Spirit*. New York: Harper Wave, 2018.

Li, Qing. *Into the Forest: How Trees Can Help You Find Health and Happiness*. London: Penguin Life, 2019.

———. *Shinrin-Yoku: The Art and Science of Forest Bathing; How Trees Can Help You Find Health and Happiness*. London: Penguin Life, 2018.

Mandela, Nelson. *Long Walk to Freedom: The Autobiography of Nelson Mandela*. Boston: Back Bay, 1995.

McCullers, Carson. *The Member of the Wedding*. Boston: Mariner, 2004.

McKeown, Patrick. *The Oxygen Advantage: The Simple, Scientifically Proven Breathing Techniques for a Healthier, Slimmer, Faster, and Fitter You*. New York: William Morrow, 2015.

Mountain Dreamer, Oriah. *The Invitation*. San Francisco: HarperSanFrancisco, 1999.

Myss, Caroline. *Anatomy of the Spirit: The Seven Stages of Power and Healing*. New York: Harmony, 2017.

Nepo, Mark. *The Book of Awakening: Having the Life You Want by Being Present to the Life You Have*. San Francisco: Conari, 2000.

Nestor, James. Breath: *The New Science of a Lost Art*. New York: Riverhead, 2020.

Ober, Clinton, Stephen T. Sinatra, and Martin Zucker. *Earthing: The Most Important Health Discovery Ever!* 2nd ed. Laguna Beach, CA: Basic Health Publications, 2014.

O'Donohue, John. *Divine Beauty: The Invisible Embrace*. London: Bantam, 2003.

Oliver, Mary. "The Summer Day." *In House of Light*, 60. Boston: Beacon, 1990.

Peace Pilgrim. *Peace Pilgrim: Her Life and Work in Her Own Words*. Compiled by some of her friends. 2nd ed. Santa Fe: Ocean Tree, 1994.

Saint-Exupéry, Antoine de. *The Little Prince*. Translated by Katherine Woods. New York: Harcourt Brace Jovanovich, 1961.

Sawatsky, Jarem. *Dancing with Elephants: Mindfulness Training for Those Living with Dementia, Chronic Illness or an Aging Brain.* Winnipeg: Red Canoe, 2017.

Severinsen, Stig. Breatheology: *The Art of Conscious Breathing.* Naples, Italy: Idelson-Gnocchi, 2010.

Stengel, Richard. *Mandela's Way: Fifteen Lessons on Life, Love, and Courage.* New York: Crown, 2010.

Vernikos, Joan. *Designed to Move: The Science-Backed Program to Fight Sitting Disease and Enjoy Lifelong Health.* Fresno, CA: Quill Driver, 2016.

Walker, Alice. *The Color Purple.* New York: Penguin, 2019.

Movies

About Time. Directed by Richard Curtis. 2013; Universal Pictures Home Entertainment, 2015. 2 hr., 3 min. Blu-ray Disc, 1080p HD.

The Best Exotic Marigold Hotel. Directed by John Madden. 2011; 20th Century Fox Home Entertainment, 2014. 2 hr., 3 min. Blu-ray Disc, 1080p HD.

Finding Joe. Directed by Patrick Takaya Solomon. 2011; Pat & Pat, 2012. 1 hr., 20 min. DVD, NTSC.

YouTube Videos

Braden, Gregg. "The Ancient Technique to Making Tough Decisions." YouTube video, 4:21. April 12, 2020. https://www.youtube.com/watch?v=exHp3L_c2Lg.

Earthing. "Down to Earth: The Earthing Movie 15 Min Short Film." YouTube video, 15:20. March 13, 2020. https://www.youtube.com/watch?v=EcHEWH8Eh0Q.

Mayo Clinic. "Sitting Disease." With James Levine. YouTube video, 13:43. August 18, 2014. https://www.youtube.com/watch?v=MfRD_a4KQoI.

Penguin Books UK. "The Art and Science of Forest Bathing with Dr Qing Li." YouTube video, 4:33. April 24, 2018. https://www.youtube.com/watch?v=12CCjoixpkA.

TED. "Nicholas Christakis: The Hidden Influence of Social Networks." TED Talk given by Nicholas Christakis in February 2020 in Long Beach, CA. YouTube video, 18:44. May 10, 2010. https://www.youtube.com/watch?v=2U-tOghblfE.

TED. "Sleep Is Your Superpower: Matt Walker." TED Talk given by Matt Walker in April 2019 in Vancouver, BC. YouTube video, 19:18. June 3, 2019. https://www.youtube.com/watch?v=5MuIMqhT8DM.

Articles

Bednar, Deanne. "Imaginal Cells: A Metaphor of Transformation." Originally published in Ecologic, Spring 2009. Available at http://strawbale.pbworks.com/w/page/18605739/Imaginal%20Cells%3A%20A%20Metaphor%20of%20Transformation.

Davis, Saskia. "Symptoms of Inner Peace™" © 1984 Author's Website http://www.symptomsofinnerpeace.net/Home.html.

"From Broken to Beautiful: The Power of Kintsugi." Concrete Unicorn, June 27, 2018. https://concreteunicorn.com/blogs/journal/from-broken-to-beautiful-the-power-of-kintsugi.

Gross, Terry and James Nestor. "How the 'Lost Art' of Breathing Can Impact Sleep and Resilience." NPR, May 27, 2020. Transcript. https://www.npr.org/transcripts/862963172.

Hani, Julie. "The Neuroscience of Behavior Change." StartUp Health, August 8, 2017. https://healthtransformer.co/the-neuroscience-of-behavior-change-bcb567fa83c1.

"How Much Screen Time Is Too Much for Adults?" Reid Blog. Reid Health, n.d. https://www.reidhealth.org/blog/screen-time-for-adults.

Levine, James. "The Chairman's Curse: Lethal Sitting." Mayo Clinic Proceedings 89, no. 8 (August 2014): 1030–32. https://www.mayoclinicproceedings.org/article/S0025-6196(14)00573-4/pdf.

Li, Qing. "'Forest Bathing' Is Great for Your Health. Here's How to Do It." Time, May 1, 2018. https://time.com/5259602/japanese-forest-bathing/.

Rosen, Zak. "Peace Pilgrim's 28-Year Walk for 'a Meaningful Way of Life.'" NPR, January 1, 2013. https://www.npr.org/2013/01/01/168346591/peace-pilgrims-28-year-walk-for-a-meaningful-way-of-life.

Sinatra, Stephen T., James L. Oschman, Gaétan Chevalier, and Drew Sinatra. "Electric Nutrition: The Surprising Health and Healing Benefits of Biological Grounding (Earthing)." Alternative Therapies in Health and Medicine 25, no. 5 (September/October 2017): 8–16. http://www.alternative-therapies.com/openaccess/electric_nutrition_the_surprising_health_and_healing_benefits_of_biological_grounding.pdf.

Theophil, Marguerite. "What Does 'Itadakimasu' Mean, Really?" Speaking Tree, October 6, 2017. https://www.speakingtree.in/article/what-does-itadakimasu-mean-really.

CPSIA information can be obtained
at www.ICGtesting.com
Printed in the USA
FSHW012032081121